Meetings, Meetings

WINSTON FLETCHER

Meetings, Meetings

How to Manipulate Them and Make Them More Fun

Michael Joseph: London

To C.H. Craddock

First published in Great Britain by Michael Joseph Ltd
44 Bedford Square, London WC1
1983

ISBN 0 7181 2295 X

Printed in Great Britain by
Hollen Street Press Ltd at Slough
and bound by Hunter and Foulis Ltd
Edinburgh, Scotland

Contents

PART ONE:

Points of Order

1

Agenda

It is, when you think about it, astonishing how cocksure most of us are about meetings.

We treat them – as we would never treat tennis, golf or horseriding, let alone accountancy or computer programming – as though they can be mastered without training or guidance, or even much forethought.

Occasionally, departing from some debacle during which we have been derisively defeated, we suffer a moment's despondency, and briefly face the distasteful fact that we are less instinctively skilful than we had fondly imagined.

Then, shrugging it off, we blame our stars rather than ourselves – and rush to the next meeting.

Almost nobody will ever admit they enjoy meetings, yet almost everybody attends them incessantly.

It's one of life's most mysterious paradoxes.

We go to meetings because
* we feel lonely working on our own
* we are scared of decisions being taken in our absence
* it makes us feel important

* we want a rest from our real work
* we want to offload the responsibility for a difficult decision
* we particularly like the sound of our own voices
* or – most frequently of all – simply because the meeting happens to be happening.

Whatever the reason, you can bet a chairman's gavel to three well-chewed pencils that after almost every meeting almost everyone will leave moaning and groaning that it's been a bloody waste of time.

Funnily enough, nobody knows how much time mankind wastes in meetings. Nobody even knows how much time mankind *spends* in meetings.

Indeed, considering the proportion of our existence which most of us devote to meetings – business meetings, leisure meetings, club meetings, political meetings, you name them – few of us know much about meetings at all.

Yet during recent years social psychologists have carried out voluminous and profound researches into how people behave in meetings; researches which the rest of us have nonchalantly neglected to study.

Doubtless we've all been too busy going to meetings.

Our unanimously equivocal feelings about meetings (and committees) have been reflected in the comments of wise men throughout the ages.

For example Sharu S. Rangnekar, in *The Art of Avoiding Decisions*, wrote:

'If you can avoid a decision, do so.

'If you can get somebody else to avoid a decision, don't avoid it yourself.
'If you cannot get one person to avoid the decision, appoint a committee.'

A point confirmed by Fred Allen:

'A committee is a gathering of important people who singly can do nothing, but together can decide that nothing can be done.'

Also by scientist Sir Barnett Cocks:

'A committee is a cul de sac down which ideas are lured and then quietly strangled.'

And even by Professor J.K. Galbraith:

'Meetings are indispensable when you don't want to do anything.'

While Richard Harkness, in the New York *Herald Tribune* in 1960, put the point somewhat differently:

'What is a committee? A group of the unwilling, picked from the unfit, to do the unnecessary.'

Or, as William H. Whyte Jr so succinctly said in his management classic *The Organization Man*:

'People very rarely think in groups; they talk together, they exchange information, they adjudicate, they make compromises. But they do not think.'

Moreover, Whyte went on:

'Any really new idea affronts current agreement – it wouldn't be a new idea if it didn't – and meetings, impelled as they are to agree, are instinctively hostile to that which is divisive.'

Happily, on one thing all the luminaries concur: the essence of a committee is its size. To quote Herbert V. Prochnow:

'The usefulness of a meeting is in inverse proportion to the attendance.'

Though it was the indefatigable Sharu S. Rangnekar who discovered the exact mathematical correlation:

'The possibility of avoiding decisions increases in proportion to the square of the number of members on the committee.'

In a spirit of healthy scientific controversy however, Rangnekar's hypothesis has been disputed by no less an authority than Professor Cyril Northcote Parkinson, who denies the squared members' correlation, but claims with unequivocal finality:

'The point of total ineffectiveness in a committee is reached when the total membership exceeds twenty.'

In a further major breakthrough, Eileen Shanahan of the *New York Times* succeeded in relating the size of meetings to the fourth dimension:

'The length of a meeting rises with the square of the number of people present – '

To which she added, confirming Rangnekar's correlation:

' – and the productivity of the meeting falls with the square of the number of people present.'

Second in importance to the size of the committee, the luminaries broadly agree, is its agenda. To quote Professor Parkinson again:

'The time spent on any item in the agenda will be in inverse proportion to the sum of money involved.'

This, as it happens, is but a descendant of a much earlier discovery by Gresham:

'In committees trivial matters are handled promptly, important matters are never solved.'

Returning to agendas, it was Dean Thomas L. Martin of the Southern Methodist University in Dallas whose pioneering work first revealed the principle which now bears his name:

'Of all possible committee reactions to any given agenda item, that one will occur which will liberate the greatest amount of hot air.'

All of these important laws were superseded in 1971 by Dr E.R. Hendrickson, President of Environmental Engineering Incorporated and discoverer of the all-embracing, all-revealing Hendrickson's Law:

'If you have enough meetings over a long enough period of time, the meetings become more important than the problem they were intended to solve.'

With which worldly words of wisdom being taken as read, let us call ourselves to order and commence.

2

Briefing

The known mathematical facts about meetings are few. Here is a brief briefing which you can quickly scan and digest before the proceedings properly get going.

A *Harvard Business Review* study showed that the average executive spends three and a half hours weekly in formal committees; and that the average committee comprises eight executives, each of whom wishes that at least three of the other seven weren't on it.

In addition, the average executive spends another full day a week in informal conferences and consultations.

Worse, in a survey of 160 British managers, Rosemary Stewart showed that they spend about half their time in formal or informal discussions, and that senior people spend more time thus than juniors.

(This seems to be widely accepted. When asked what British cabinet ministers do all day, Prime Minister Harold Wilson replied, 'They go to meetings.')

Consultant James Rice, who studied meetings in one hundred large UK firms, estimates that not more than one in ten of them works efficiently.

This roughly corroborates another study's finding that nine out of ten businessmen believe half the time they spend in meetings to be wasted.

Confirming the Harvard study of executives' subjective feelings, a large number of experimental studies have shown five to be the optimum number of participants for a productive meeting. Researcher A.P. Hare, for example, proved – less than astonishingly – that groups of five take less time to make decisions than groups of twelve.

(It is well established that governmental committees and meetings tend to be far larger than those in business. No comment.)

It has been estimated that every day of the year 11 million meetings are held in the United States alone. That figure extrapolates into a conservative guestimate of 50 million daily meetings in the world.

In his seminal study *The Effects of Co-operation and Competition Upon Group Process*, M. Deutsch threw abundant cold water upon the theory of creative friction (page 14) in meetings.

He showed that internally co-operative groups are more productive and more effective than internally competitive groups; that co-operative groups actually generate a greater individual motivation to complete group tasks; and that co-operative groups more successfully create systems for the division of labour; they are also a lot more enjoyable. These findings have broadly been confirmed by other researchers.

Company managements and similar hierarchies frequently form their subordinates into committees in the belief that the group members will act as restraining checks and balances upon each other.

Wrong.

Contrary to common belief, many experiments have proved that groups arrive at riskier decisions than individuals do alone.

This phenomenon, now known as the Risky Shift Effect, was first identified by psychologists N. Kogan and M.A. Wallach in their 1967 paper *Risk-taking as a function of the situation, the person and the group*.

Kogan and Wallach's work was supported by MIT graduate James Stoner's studies of decision-making among a large number of groups: in almost all cases, the decisions made by individuals on their own were more conservative than those made by the same individuals when they acted together.

Following Stoner, several other social psychologists researched the subject and repeatedly confirmed his findings.

Kogan and Wallach suggested that Risky Shifts resulted from the diffusion of responsibility among group members: when no one is personally responsible, it's safe for everyone to gamble.

Other researchers have hypothesized that our cultural norms encourage risk-taking; still others believe that within groups the individuals who are prone to take risks exert most influence on the others.

Whatever the explanation, the cliché that committees

create conservative compromises is clearly contradicted by the facts.

If 'A camel is a horse designed by a committee', then the committee was probably gambling recklessly on an exceedingly dry summer.

Finally, the role of chairman, which we'll investigate in greater detail in chapter 7.

Far more has been written about how chairmen should and should not run meetings than about any other aspect of meeting behaviour.

This seems odd because, as we have seen, there are seven times as many non-chairmen as chairmen at the average meeting.

Clearly, this spotlights the widespread belief that an effective chairman is crucial to an effective meeting.

Without seeking to deny the importance of good chairmen, let's beg to differ.

The vast majority of *ad hoc* meetings – between buyers and suppliers, between advisors and advised, among project groups and problem solvers – have no chairman and need no chairman.

Perhaps that's why so many are so often so simple to manipulate.

3

Terms of Reference

For our purposes, meetings will be defined as gatherings of three to twenty people lasting fifteen minutes or more.

Larger groups become conferences, smaller or shorter groupings hardly constitute proper meetings.

(Though the law, as we shall see, does not agree.)

Meetings can be, and frequently are, classified, categorized and analysed in any number of ways.

Certain types of meeting – annual general meetings, for example – may enjoy specific status, authority and responsibilities, either legal or constitutional (in a club or political party).

Fundamentally and colloquially however, meetings come in two basic forms:

The Committee: regular, formalized, structured, usually with a chairman and other functionaries.

The Get-together: informal, spontaneous or semi-spontaneous, usually lacking nominated functionaries and frequently lacking any clearly stated objectives.

Committees normally have long multi-subject agendas.
Get-togethers are more often devoted to single issues,
even if the issue is subdivided into many facets.

Only the most optimistic (destined for eternal
disappointment) and the most naive (impervious to harsh
reality) believe that the prime purpose of meetings is to
reach conclusions and make decisions.

Social psychologist A.A. Harrison, in *Individuals and
Groups*, listed the five purposes of meetings as follows:

* the pooling of skills and resources
* division of labour
* group members can stimulate each other
* members may be made more considerate of others'
  problems
* members can encourage and support each other.

Harrison then added four disadvantages, with which
regular meeting-goers will doubtless be more familiar:

* there are frequently conflicts among members
* social norms and conformity destroy novel ideas
* people are reluctant to speak because they fear negative
  evaluations from others
* people in groups either argue or have fun and so devote
  less time to the task in hand than do individuals working
  separately.

From your own narrow, personal point of view – which is
after all what *Meetings, Meetings* is about – the functions
of meetings can be eightfold:

1.   Information communication
You will sometimes be forced to present data in writing:

do so as rarely as possible; the ideal way to present data is verbally or on charts, either of which provides you with maximum control of the meeting and provides everyone else with the minimum opportunity to spot your errors. When others are presenting information remember our First Law of Meetings: **all data is suspect; verbal data is more suspect than written data; top-of-the-head data produced in meetings is most suspect of all.**

2. Impression creation
'For a young man on the make there is no better vehicle than the conference way. Where fifty years before he might have had to labour unseen by all but his immediate superior, now via the conference he can expose himself to all sorts of superiors across the line of command. Given minimum committeemanship skills, by an adroit question here and a modest suggestion there, he can call attention to himself and still play the game.'

William H. Whyte Jr, *The Organization Man*

3. Participant evaluation
Whatever the age of the participant, the converse of 2 is also true. We'll explore this more in chapter 4.

4. Inspiration generation
Whether in an officially-designated-free-wheeling-think-tank session, or simply in general conclave, you may be one of those people who finds it easier to resolve problems and originate solutions by bickering with others; this process is known either as creative friction or, more accurately, as natural human cussedness – in any event, its efficacy is more than somewhat questionable.

5. Idea flotation
Meetings are perfect occasions to test the temperature of other people's reactions to your ideas, prior to putting

them forward with greater commitment (i.e., on paper); but beware of researcher Robert F. Bales's finding that people who have too many ideas in meetings are unlikely to be liked by the other participants.

6.   Credit banking
Any issue about the outcome of which you don't give a paperclip offers a fine opportunity to support your friends and irritate your enemies – and, more importantly, to bank cheap 'credits' which can be cashed in later (not necessarily within the meeting) for favours to be repaid.

7.   Camouflaged coercion
Frequently, the presence of onlookers can help you persuade somebody to comply with a proposal they would forcibly reject in private; this technique must be used sparingly since it provokes elephantine resentments: huge and never forgotten.

8.   Decision consummation
Lastly, meetings do sometimes reach decisions, some of which you may wish to influence. Read on.

4

Reconnaissance

Despite appearances to the contrary, meetings are not games.

(The rules are too nebulous; there is no agreed system of scoring; and it is rarely clear who, if anyone, has won.)

Nonetheless, as has previously been suggested, they share many of the characteristics of games – competitive interaction, broadly agreed procedures and a propensity for players to cheat.

Most particularly, like all games they demand both advance planning and nifty reactions once the joust is in progress.

'Be prepared' is the least exciting advice known to mankind.

But no serious player wanting to win would dream of going into a tennis or chess or football match without prior strategic thought.

Planning comes in three parts.

First, define your objectives.

This must be done in terms of the eight functions, and

highlights another significant way in which meetings differ from games.

In games all involved have the same objective: to win. In most meetings most of those present have mostly different objectives. That must forever be remembered; in the heat of a meeting, it is easy to forget.

Second, deal with the practical matters.

Read the agenda and the papers, if any. Obtain additional information – preferably information unknown to anyone else – on any points upon which you wish to make a contribution. Ensure that you are ready for solos you may be called upon to perform. Check and re-check visual aids you may be planning to use. (Kodak's Law states unequivocally that any slides which can be upside down will be upside down.) Check the time and venue of the meeting.

(There is no frequent meeting-goer in the world who has not, on occasion, found himself in the wrong place at the right time or in the right place at the wrong time.)

Dealing with these practical matters should be automatic, mechanical. Failure to cope with them is like going off to play tennis and neglecting to take sports shoes.

(Which is not to say that innumerable people do not turn up at the courts sneaker-less. This does not help them to start their game perfectly composed and confident.)

Third, and this is most fun, analyse the participants.

It is idle to attend any meeting without having made strenuous efforts to discover who will be present. This is frequently difficult and sometimes impossible.

Nonetheless time spent in reconnaissance is seldom wasted.

Once you have the list, divide it into five.

1. Those who will only speak when they have something worth saying: **the Seers**.

2. Those who will yatter incessantly: **the Talkies**.

3. Those who will utter only when they feel or fear the issue to be impinging on themselves: **the Passionates**.

4. Those who will stay silent almost throughout: **the Mums.**

5. **the Unknowns**.

There may occasionally be borderline cases, but virtually every meeting-goer can easily be thus classified. The classification is one of personality rather than role or job function; an individual's meeting style rarely varies. However, beware of Mums who transform themselves into little bitches when they move from big-fish pools in which they are petrified to pools populated by little 'uns which they can dominate.

Let's consider each group, last first.

Unless you have reason to believe any of the Unknowns are especially important – in which case investigations must be initiated immediately – do not bother about them before the meeting.

(Time is too short and meetings are too many.)

On arrival at the event keep a wary eye on them, and assign them to their rightful category – 1 to 4 – as soon as you can confidently do so.

Turning to category 4, ignore them.

The Greeks said, 'There is no wisdom like silence,' but this doesn't apply in meetings.

It is sad and cruel but – unless it is one of those rare assemblies where a vote will be taken – ninety-nine times out of a hundred people who stay Mum can safely be forgotten.

(The exception being the Mum whom you may wish to impress. However, it is likewise sad and cruel, but those who are voiceless are rarely those whom you wish to impress.)

For different reasons, the Passionates are hardly worth worrying about either.

Everyone generally knows the issues about which the Passionates are passionate long before the meeting begins, it being the nature of Passionates to make their views known.

Should any of these issues matter to you, you will need to know where each Passionate stands, since the Second Law of Meetings states that **Passionates are both more persuasive and less persuadable than anyone else.**

Even the inarticulate will burst into eloquent oratory on issues about which they care fervently; it can be most disconcerting. Corollary to the Second Law: canvassing Passionates is either timewasting, if they agree with you; or counter-productive, if they don't.

Which is why there is no point in bothering them at this stage.

NB: Passionates are more frequently against than for any course of action. If several are united (itself a rare event) in opposition to a cause you yourself hold dear, then –

unless you are in an especially masochistic mood – forget it.

Because Passionates occasionally burst into vociferous flame, do not be misled into believing that they are emotional; on the contrary, they tend to relapse into a placid day-dreaming stupor whenever they are not personally involved.

Talkies, on the other hand, are well worth canvassing. (It should not be assumed that all Talkies are windbags. It is not quite an inviolable law but most often, in meetings, those who say most are those who have most worth saying.) If you suspect that you will need support on any issue, Talkies are usually malleable. If you wish to know what line the meeting will take on any issue, the Talkies will be able to offer an informed guess. If you wish to plant an argument, rather than voice it yourself, Talkies can usually be relied upon to do the job – knowingly or otherwise.

Psychologist N.R.F. Maier has shown that solutions to problems will be accepted and adopted by groups when they have been put forward by the most talkative member. Robert F. Bales's researches arrived at the same conclusion, which was finally proven beyond question by Henry W. Riesken in his study *The Effect of Talkativeness on Ability to Influence Group Solutions*.

Hence, if you are not a Talkie yourself – and indeed even if you are – Talkies make the best meeting allies.

There is a sub-group of Talkies, famed in meeting mythology, who are indeed just garrulous Windbags.

In reality, there are far fewer Windbags than is commonly supposed. First, because only a minority of human beings can withstand the pained, withering stares of their colleagues.

Second, because quite quickly everyone in an organization gets to know who they are and desperately avoids inviting them to meetings.

Still, they do exist, and nothing that has been said about real Talkies applies to them.

Finally, the Seers.

The category to which all of us would like to belong, and most of us believe we do.

Seers are characteristically of little help to others.

They are not malleable. They prefer to play their cards close to their chest. They hate to commit themselves before they need to. They don't gossip. They hardly ever make good allies.

Clever men, D.H. Lawrence noted, are unpleasant animals.

None of which is intended to imply that they may not be powerfully influential at the forum itself; merely that in terms of meeting manipulation they are of little use to you.

Having analysed the participants, the final crucial preliminary meeting activity is the Pre-Mix, known to politicians as the Lobby.

In politics, especially in American politics, most of the vitally important decisions made in meetings are not made in the meetings at all.

They are made beforehand in caucuses and on the telephone.

Tales of Westminster and Washington overflow with deals and dalliances, pacts and compacts, understandings and undertakings, concordats and conspiracies – all settled long before the meetings that were supposed to settle them ever met.

The same thing happens of course, on a lowlier level and to a lesser extent, in companies, clubs and institutions of every kind.

Those who love intrigue will lobby and plot to rig the results, rather than risk decisions which may not be to their liking.

Politicians play the Pre-Mix game effortlessly, naturally; not to do so seems strange to them.

However, in other walks of life you must be more circumspect.

In the first place, as we've seen, not everyone either likes to be or can be lobbied.

In the second, politicians who have been clandestinely lobbied are marvellous at hiding the fact – I've watched politicians act their way through meetings like Bancroft Gold Medallists at RADA; but few of us are such accomplished actors and, once the gaff is blown, the Pre-Mix self-destructs.

Third, if you gain a reputation as a plotter your credibility can become tarnished beyond repair (see Trust Me, page 175).

Then people will call you a politician – than which, in meetings, few designations are more derogatory.

5

The Seven Deadly Skills

Before progressing further it is important to consider here the seven basic forms of effective meeting behaviour. In alphabetical order: **Aggression, Conciliation, Enthusiasm, Interrogation, Patience, Sulks** and **Withdrawal.**

(Any successful meeting-goer needs at least a smidgen of theatricality in his blood.)

As ever, you must assess roughly how you intend to behave throughout the proceedings, in line with your objectives, before the congregation assembles; then you must adjust as circumstances dictate.

'There are no straight roads in the world,' Mao said, 'if you wish to get from A to B it is necessary to twist and turn.'

AGGRESSION
Psychologists differentiate between *angry* aggression and *instrumental* aggression (aggression designed to gain a specific goal).

In meetings, angry aggression must be strictly *verboten*; instrumental aggression should be employed sparely but often.

What form should meeting aggression take? Palpably it must be verbal rather than physical, of which the corollary is that it must be threatening rather than real.

Tone of voice and subtle use of body language (chapter 6) normally suffice. When you sound furious, people believe that you *are* furious. Indeed, psychological researches have shown that, if you make yourself look angry, you will quickly make yourself *feel* angry.

Professor Erving Goffman demonstrated in *The Presentation of Self in Everyday Life* that, in order to perform a new role effectively, individuals put on a 'mask'; when the mask has been worn for long enough, it becomes part of the personality and is thus no longer a mask.

A phenomenon with which regular meeting-goers will be all too familiar.

A simple aggressive tip: it is almost impossible for two human beings to indulge in simultaneous speech for more than a few seconds. Our neurophysiological make-up prevents us from imparting our own information and decoding someone else's at the same time. Keep talking.

Outright threats, however – 'I'll get you fired', 'I'll smash your face in' – are almost invariably counter-productive: they can virtually never be effected; they win onlookers' support for the person being threatened; they are embarrassing; they make you appear both desperate and foolish. (Remember we have defined meetings as comprising at least three people.)

Threats should be oblique and nebulous. The classic Hollywood clichés – 'Don't think you've heard the end of this', 'Just watch what you're saying', and the rest – rarely fail.

Swear words are fine, in moderation.

Never call people liars. Hint strongly that they are lying.

Avoid personal insults.

Where appropriate, which is usually, keep in mind that you will still need to work with your antagonist after the meeting.

Never ever admit afterwards that your anger was simulated; otherwise it will be disregarded in future.

Robert F. Bales's studies showed aggression in meetings to be surprisingly uncommon: well under 1 per cent of all statements 'show antagonism'.

That is why, adroitly used, it is so effective.

(See the Full Frontal, page 127.)

Everybody admires, though few like, people who are aggressive in meetings.

Much of which was succinctly summed up in 1836 by Henry Taylor in his classic guidebook to diplomacy *The Statesman*:

> 'For a statesman should be by nature and temper the most unquarrelsome of men, and when he finds it necessary to quarrel, should do it, though with a stout heart, with a cool head. There is no such test of a man's superiority of character as in the well-conducting of an unavoidable quarrel.'

CONCILIATION

Conciliation is an underrated weapon in the
meeting-goer's armoury.

Konrad Lorenz has shown that an aggressive animal can
be pacified by appeasement signals and submissive
postures.

Likewise, in meetings aggressors can be both defused and
confused by overtly conciliatory behaviour.

As with aggression, conciliation must be employed
sparingly.

The more forceful you are most of the time the more
surprising, and effective, your occasional apologies and
admissions of error will be.

The single most powerful conciliatory stratagem – which
is chronicled on pages 140–44 – is the Pre-emptive
Apology ('It's My Fault It's Your Fault'). Like pleading
guilty in court, it takes all wind from the prosecutor's sails
and guillotines further haranguing.

Less frequently usable conciliatory techniques include:

The overkill self-punishment: 'OK, fire me then, kick me
round the room if it will make you feel better.'

(In *Games People Play*, Dr Eric Berne indeed calls his
equivalent of this manoeuvre Kick Me.)

Meetings should never be treated as confessionals;
nonetheless, the judicious use of a *mea culpa* can be relied
upon to absolve you from too much admonishment.

The invincible sympathy-builder: I once worked for an

unlovable entrepreneur who, whenever he was unable or unwilling to pay his bills, would imply strongly that he was suffering from cancer. 'Can't discuss the matter now. Off to hospital. Prefer not to talk about it ... but the radium treatment is terribly, terribly painful.'

Few human beings are prepared to gamble so outrageously with fate; but similar results can be achieved from less extreme sympathy-builders.

We're none of us perfect: The use of socially acceptable inadequacies ('I'm afraid maybe I had had a drop too much to drink ...') at which few have the temerity to cast the first stone.

Dr Berne's version is called Wooden Leg and he describes its most dramatic form as the Plea of Insanity. This runs as follows: 'What do you expect of someone as emotionally disturbed as I am – that I would refrain from killing people?' To which the jury is asked to reply, 'Certainly not, we would hardly impose that restriction on you!'

'The businessman,' wrote H.L. Mencken, 'is the only man who is forever apologizing for his occupation.'

Maybe he spends so much of his time in meetings that he gets addicted to self-mortification.

ENTHUSIASM
Whereas, as has been said, both aggression and conciliation have scarcity value, enthusiasm is something of which you can hardly have too much.

The Third Law of Meetings – an offspring of Eileen Shanahan's rule (page 6) – states that **the soporific content of any meeting is proportional to the square of its length.**

(From which it is not possible to deduce that shorter meetings are invariably exhilarating. No such luck.)

Corollary to the Third Law: anyone with the resilience to stay perky will frequently be able to put one over on the other participants when they are comatose or even asleep.

Second corollary to the Third Law: most enthusiasts are Talkies whom, as has already been seen, have a high propensity to win points and influence others.

Moreover, enthusiasts are almost always popular at meetings.

Psychologists have offered no explanation of this phenomenon. My own hypothesis is that most of us are so exhausted and emasculated by the unending flow of interminable convocations that we are both impressed and delighted by the gallant few with sufficient surplus energy to keep up a state of perpetual enthusiasm.

It assuages our guilt feelings (and allows us another little clandestine kip).

Two minor warnings for enthusiasts:

First, enthusiasm must not be confused with mere loquacity (see Windbags, page 20). True enthusiasm involves the continuous innovation of ideas and arguments, not the repetitious plodding-on of hobby horses.

Second, even the true enthusiast must eschew the ever-present danger of becoming too dominant. Parry and thrust – rather than monologue and filibuster – must be the enthusiast's motto: to achieve which it could even be necessary to awaken one or two of the other participants from time to time, unwelcome though this may be to them.

INTERROGATION

Don't you frequently feel that many meeting-goers are far cleverer than you at asking cunning questions?

They use questions to delay decisions, incite arguments, prick pomposity and – most ingeniously of all – as statements in disguise.

(We are not here referring to so-called rhetorical questions, which are not really questions at all. True questions demand, and gain their strength from, the answers they provoke.)

Delaying decisions is of course kidstuff:

'Surely we'd better wait till we get all the facts . . .?'

'Do we really dare go ahead without consulting . . .?'

'Hadn't we better consider all the consequences in depth before finally . . .?'

Etc., etc., etc.

Inciting arguments is hardly harder:

'Are you actually trying to claim that . . .?'

'How can we rely on that in the light of your past . . .?'

'I don't wish to sound distrustful, but are you absolutely certain . . .?'

Occasionally it is useful, or anyway fun, to incite an argument among others with a transferred question:

'Personally, I don't feel strongly about this, but how can you ignore Harry's basic criticism, Bill . . .?'

'Surely what Charles is trying to say, isn't he, John, is that your report is complete and utter . . .?'

After which, having lit the touchpaper, it is sensible to retire to a safe silence.

Transferred questions can also be used to elicit information you want but do not want everyone to know you want.

I attended a seven-day international business meeting at which a wily old Australian delegate deployed this technique brilliantly; it wasn't until day three, when happening to sit next to him, that I twigged.

Incomprehensible chart No. 73, overflowing with data like most of its predecessors, was presented to the meeting.

It appeared to be comparing various countries' business performances, and Canada was beating Australia into second place.

The Aussie leaned towards me.

'Don't those Canadian figures look suspicious to you, mate?' he whispered. 'D'you know whether they've added on their US export sales which shouldn't be included?'

'No,' I replied truthfully; there was no way I could possibly have known.

'Winston here thinks that chart's a bit suspicious and he wants to know,' the Aussie then said loudly, 'whether Canada has included US export sales . . . ?'

This immediately prompted other delegates whose countries were not shown to be doing too well to raise similar defensive questions; hubbub ensued. By the time the situation was clarified, the chart had been completely discredited; and the Aussie sat smiling seraphically throughout.

Questions can also be used to prick pomposity. This was a particular pleasure of the late Stephen Potter, President of the Lifemanship Correspondence College.

In an all-too-brief chapter on 'Committeeship' in his seminal work *One-Upmanship* he includes such sharp deflaters as:

'Yes, but don't let's forget the big picture. What after all are you trying to sell?'

'Yes, but that isn't really what we're discussing, is it?'

'Well, there are definite reasons why that is going to become impracticable fairly shortly, aren't there?'

Or:

'Yes, I think that's a good idea – I wonder if we were right to discard it five years ago when there was all that row?'

(Note the disarming use of the affirmative opening 'Yes', or 'Well', which sure-footedly pre-empts any combative riposte.)

However, it is as camouflaged statements that questions truly come into their own.

First, uncertain (or invented) data can invariably be more safely incorporated into inquiries than propagated as fact:

> 'Surely that was in August 1973?... Or was it in Vladivostock?... Don't we normally achieve an average of 17.65 per cent on jobs of this type?... Wasn't it Smithson-Clarke who was caught with his secretary in the stationery cupboard?'

Second, questions – usually phrased negatively – can covertly transfer responsibilities (and thence blame):

> 'Do you mean you just don't care about the state of the loos?... Aren't you at all interested in whether we win the contract?... Doesn't it worry you if the building is completely unsafe?'

Respondent is in every case forced to answer 'Yes ...', thus ineluctably accepting some measure of responsibility for the problem.

Third, by assuming what they are seeking to prove, questions can be accusatory in the time-honoured legal tradition:

> 'When did you stop beating your wife?'

With a little practice, mastering this trick is easy as doodling:

'Why do you so frequently arrive late?... Why is it
there's nearly always a mistake in the plans?... How
many times have you forgotten that?'

It's the use of an indefinite quantification – how often, so
frequently, etc. – which (almost invariably) makes such
questions (all but) impossible to challenge.

If accusatory questions are pushed to their limit, they can
maliciously smear opponents beyond redemption.

The divisional managing director of one of the country's
largest electrical engineering groups would use them
ruthlessly to avoid employing any supplier of whom he
disapproved.

'I don't suppose there's any chance that you or one of
your team is getting a kickback from X in return for this
contract, is there?' was his best-loved smear.

Rebutting the allegation – which could never have been
put forward as a statement, but was devastating as a
question – would have been difficult enough in private; at
a meeting, with watchful onlookers radiating
there's-no-smoke-without-fire suspicions, the accused
would either remain (guiltily) silent or protest too much.

Inevitably, in order finally to disprove the existence of any
such secret hanky-panky, the supplier would be dropped.

As the late US Senator Joe Are-you-now-or-have-you-
ever-been? McCarthy proved, tactical smear questions
aren't lovely but they can be lethal.

The finely phrased question is indeed the most flexible of
friends.

Yet, surprisingly, few meeting-goers employ interrogation effectively.

Robert F. Bales showed that only 7 per cent of all meeting utterances were questions. Of these, 50 per cent were straightforward requests for further information, 34 per cent were requests for views and opinions, and a minority 16 per cent – just over 1 per cent of total utterances – were doubtless optimistic pleas for suggestions and ideas.

Mark Twain demonstrated that any antagonist can be reduced to frustrated, fumbling stupefaction by the persistent and repeated probe 'Why?...Why?...Why?'

It works because few of us can resist attempting to answer seemingly simple queries – often to our detriment.

One of the most manipulative meetings men I have encountered would lob out his questions loudly, like a schoolteacher, to everyone present:

> 'Can anyone tell me how sales are going in Birmingham?... Does anybody here know the precise cost of putting the cap on the tube?... Who can name the date when supplies will be ready?'

An inability to answer implied, just as it did at school, idle ignorance.

On the other hand, an enthusiastic response immediately generated a barrage of follow-up supplementaries.

(If your question is a genuine inquiry, rather than a camouflaged statement, you should always be ready to fling an incisive supplementary or two, as MPs do in Parliamentary Question Time).

Don't you think you would almost always be more
successful in meetings if you taught yourself to be far
cleverer at asking cunning questions?

PATIENCE

'How poor are they that have not patience.' (*Othello*)

Though not himself – so far as is known – a dedicated
meeting-goer, Shakespeare was spot-on as always.

Contrary to popular belief, few successful people are
impatient.

(This is not to say that they do not frequently employ
impatience as a form of instrumental aggression.)

Richard Buskirk, in his *Handbook of Management
Tactics*, quotes a great American lawyer thus:

> 'In all my legal experience with business, probably the
> most important virtue a good businessman can have is
> *patience*. Many things simply take time and the man
> who is impatient inevitably commits mistakes to his
> disadvantage.'

Inexcusably, people who are by nature impatient usually
excuse their hasty temperament self-indulgently: 'I've
always been impetuous and there's nothing I can do about
it.'

Piffle.

It is transparently true that no amount of self-discipline
will turn a fiery Talkie into a quiescent Seer. Nonetheless,
control can restrain rashness a little; and in meetings
every little counts.

Momentary digression: alcohol fuels impatience. If you're a hothead prone to a lunchtime tipple, try, try and try again to fix your important meetings in the mornings.

Patience must never, however, be confused with timidity.

The purpose of patience is to postpone in order to win, not to take the line of least resistance and lose.

Fabian tactics, invented by the great Roman general Quintus Fabius, demand that you do not rush headlong into the battlefield but take your time, pick your moment, and win skirmishes.

A sound strategy for most meetings.

(See both the Full Frontal and Red Herrings, pages 127 and 161).

Patience allows you to listen to the arguments advanced by other combatants, perceive who is on whose side, and prepare your own case as effectively as possible.

It also, incidentally, allows you ample opportunity to make speechnotes. Many, if not most, successful meeting-goers jot down speechnotes before bursting into apparently *ad hoc* oratory.

When, then, is it right to strike?

Timing is an inborn talent, though one that must be honed by experience.

There are occasions when speed is of the essence, when a pre-emptive strike can clinch a decision by nipping discussion in the bud.

Such occasions are far rarer in meetings than they are in battle.

To succeed, they demand, as in battle, advanced planning and a detailed knowledge of the strengths, weaknesses and dispositions of any likely enemies.

'More haste less speed' might have been coined specifically to describe the outcome of precipitate pre-emptive moves in meetings.

Generally, the best advice that can be given is: wait as late as you dare, but never risk allowing the decision to be taken, or the chairman calling the subject closed. Re-opening a decision or discussion is often impossible, and anyway always so irritating to the other meeting members as to be almost inevitably counter-productive.

Perhaps the greatest meeting art is to reconcile those two seemingly irreconcilable skills: patience and enthusiasm.

If you are sceptical as to whether it can be done, watch any great tennis player.

When you can do it yourself, you're well on your way to winning.

SULKS

Your use of sulks must be rationed rigorously; frequent sulking rapidly depreciates its impact. You become known as a moaner, and ignored.

Only withdrawal, the seventh and last deadly skill, has more scarcity value.

Sulking works far better in small meetings than in larger

ones, and obviously is of no use whatsoever unless it is noticeable and noticed.

Sulking must never be self-piteous, a whining wallow in wounded pride.

Its sole aim is to elicit sympathy.

Much as it may astonish you, copious evidence exists that human beings are naturally sympathetic creatures.

Well, they are when correctly prodded.

As long ago as 1937, psychologist L.B. Murphy showed that two- to five-year-old children comfort each other when upset, and help each other against an aggressive third child.

(Though note that a child quickly abandons its sympathetic behaviour in favour of egocentric behaviour if the other child's activities interfere with its own interests!)

D.O. Hebb in his authoritative *Textbook of Psychology* concludes that 'altruism is a product of evolution and not something that must be beaten into the human child because of the needs of society'.

Berkowitz and Daniels in 1964 demonstrated that people give more help to those whom they believe to be dependent on them.

Hence the value of sad sulking.

Nor is it the case, as cynics might suspect, that people only help others in the hope of self-reward; numerous field studies and laboratory experiments have proved the contrary.

(Though, in meetings, a strong hint of I'll-scratch-your-back-if-you-scratch-mine rarely goes entirely amiss.)

We'll discuss the use of body language more fully in the next chapter, but meanwhile remember that, when simulating sulks to stimulate sympathy, most people control their mouths much more successfully than their eyes – as Paul Ekman and Wallace Friesen first proved in 1967. It is silly to give the game away by sulking with one orifice while smiling with two others.

A discrepancy which, psychological researchers have shown, is more likely to be noticed by women than men – since women are generally better at perceiving accurately what other people are feeling.

How should you exploit sympathies thus skilfully won?

Above all, as a means of short-term credit banking (page 15).

Very, very few meeting-people like to kick a fellow meeting-person when he's down; even fewer wish to be seen to do so.

(Yet another way in which meetings are unlike true games.)

Thus it is often worth sulkily sacrificing a point that is trivial to you in order to gain sufficient sympathy to win a subsequent argument you care about.

It's like sacrificing a pawn in Chess or a trick in Bridge.

This is so useful and significant a meeting manoeuvre that it constitutes the Fourth Law of Meetings: **win worthwhile victories by exploiting worthless defeats**.

When the boot is on the other foot, however, beware: always keep a wary eye open for experienced meeting-goers – particularly Talkies and Seers – who may themselves be preparing a lethal torpedo by building up sympathy agin' you.

In meetings when everyone is pretending to be nice, things can get pretty nasty.

WITHDRAWAL

Before reaching withdrawal – *committeus interruptus*, as it might be called – we must briefly deal with another meeting style which perennially provides the prelude – the foreplay, as it might be called – to a climactic departure.

Stubbornness.

Being stubborn demands no skill – just bloody-mindedness and thick skin.

To deploy stubbornness successfully you need to hold some power, or anyway significant influence, in the meeting. Obdurate juniors are rapidly overruled.

Talkies and Mums are generally less mulish than Passionates and Seers. (Though in the case of Mums – and this is their problem – how can you tell?) Like aggression and sulks, stubbornness must be used sparingly.

Nonetheless, 'He can be pretty pig-headed when he likes' is invariably a complimentary description.

Put the other way around, it's a blinding glimpse of the obvious: anybody who is never stubborn is feeble.

George Bernard Shaw put the point pungently in *Man and Superman*:

> 'The reasonable man adapts himself to suit the world, while the unreasonable man seeks to adjust the world to suit him. Therefore, all progress depends upon the unreasonable man.'

Indeed, in adversary negotiation (chapter 11) we shall see that unreasonable cussedness is part of the art.

None of this is a recommendation to be randomly intransigent.

It is crucial to choose carefully those issues on which you intend to be unbending.

Those who defend the indefensible quickly become known as the meetings' equivalent of party-poopers: nobody invites them to their meetings.

(Of course, if that is your aim, persistent perverse obstinacy is an exhilaratingly cathartic way to achieve it.)

Unimpeachable grounds on which to be stubborn are:

Morality: insisting that your opponents' case is ethically despicable puts you in an almost cast-iron position.

Costs: keep sceptically questioning, and re-questioning, the quoted costs.

Practicality: 'it cannot be done in the time/in the way proposed/at all'.

Misinformation: in meetings there is no such thing as an indisputable fact.

Integrity: either impugn the integrity of your antagonist ('I wouldn't like to suggest that you have a personal financial interest in this, Ralph . . .') or, in desperate situations, lay your own integrity on the line ('I myself simply cannot be party to this decision . . .').

Which brings us, at last, to withdrawal.

You hardly need a doctorate in Business Studies to know that you can, mathematically, withdraw only once per meeting; and, sensibly, only once every few months at the most.

(This excludes brief tactical withdrawals, to go to the loo or make phone calls, which neatly timed can throw a meeting – and more particularly your opposition – into confusion and disarray. See Sorry It's Urgent, page 69, and The Sprint, page 172.)

Nor patently, once again, will your exodus matter a jot unless you hold some power or significant influence over the subject in debate.

Withdrawal being a high-risk action, it should only be employed for high rewards, never fooled about with.

Keep in mind your objective: before leaving you have presumably fought, and are running away to live to fight another day.

So that, if the meeting goes against you in your absence, your exit will have been fruitless.

It is generally too risky to withdraw if:

* the meeting or committee has a strong chairman

* a colleague, boss or even subordinate may feel, under pressure from others at the meeting, that they can 'speak for you'

* most of those present will suspect you to have been motivated by pique rather than by principle.

It is thus fairly safe to leave in all of the opposite situations:

* the meeting has a weak chairman or better still no leader at all

* nobody else will dare speak on your behalf

* everyone will believe you to be acting from principle rather than pique.

Guidelines apart, it is essential to think through, as diligently and percipiently as you know how, what will happen in the meeting after your departure.

Remember that, if you have clumsily misused one of the other six skills, you can later try to correct your bloomer. Once you have fled the proceedings, you've had it.

*   *   *

Having analysed the people and the basic skills necessary to deal with them, the next three chapters delve in detail into three inescapable aspects of meeting life: body language, chairmanship and meeting law.

If you want to manipulate meetings, you'll need to master them all.

6

Sounds of Silence

Charm schools, drama schools, Emily Post, and army drill sergeants since the dawn of time have always been well aware of the eloquence of non-verbal communication.

Yet only during the last three decades has body language been studied scientifically.

Appearance, posture, bearing, movement, expressions: those are the raw material of the new science called 'kinesics'.

Its gurus are Professors Albert Schlefen, Michael Argyle and Ray Birdwhistell – who once spent over a hundred hours analysing a few seconds' conversation between two people which he had recorded on slow-motion film.

They have invented a nauseous cornucopia of jargon including 'metabehaviour', 'prepsychodynamic', 'proxemics' and 'parallel schizmogenesis'.

Much, probably most, of their work has been devoted to human beings' amorous non-verbal communications during courtship and mating.

Sadly, that does not greatly concern us here.

Though gender differences (despite the worthy efforts of
the apostles of sexual equality) are not unimportant in
meetings.

Investigations by Scott, Gurnee and others show, less
than astonishingly, that single-sex meetings generally
work far more efficiently than those that are mixed.

Indeed, it is moronic myopia to ignore the effects of
sexual relationships in heterosexual gatherings.

I once watched one of the country's leading market
researchers, a lady who controls a large and successful
survey company, twist fourteen top businessmen round
her elegant little finger in a meeting: with deft smiles and
fluttering lashes, she conveyed to each in turn her hero-
worship and adoration.

(More bluntly, she induced each of them to believe that
she would willingly accede to their libidinous proposals if
they acceded to her business proposals. They did. She
didn't. So far as I know.)

Men rarely find themselves similarly outnumbered by
women; but males who diligently and old-fashionedly
flatter the females present win their support more often
than not.

Indeed, flattering flirtation, without complicating
consummation, is the first (and only worthwhile) rule of
heterosexual meeting manipulation.

(Dr Eric Berne, in *Games People Play*, calls this game
First Degree Rapo. Second Degree Rapo – colloquially
known as 'Buzz Off, Buster' – and vicious Third Degree
Rapo, involve much more intense emotional

entanglements and rarely surface in meetings. Not everything about meetings is bad news.)

To ensure that your Rapos never stray accidentally into unwelcome Second Degree 'Buzz Off, Busters' you must – like the lady market researcher – be even-handedly generous with your flirtatiousness.

Lavish it on all or on none. Favouritism is worse than genial indifference.

Similarly, you must watch warily for sexual *liaisons* that may be *dangereuses*: clandestine courtships, hostilities between ex-lovers, unrequited passions or chemical antipathies. Few heterosexual meetings occur in which Cupid is not at work with his little arrows somewhere.

Even in the most pompously formal of committees, if there are persons present of opposite genders sex will rear its unruly head somehow.

And, despite their utmost caution, the body language of those involved will reveal all to the perceptive observer.

How does body language work? To quote Professor Michael Argyle:

> 'Human relationships are established, developed and maintained mainly by non-verbal signals, although of course words are also used . . . We are only partly aware of non-verbal signals from others, we are hardly ever aware of the signals we are sending ourselves. These non-verbal signals constitute a silent language which, although they may be the more important aspect of an encounter, operate largely outside the focus of constant attention.'

Example: as Argyle and four colleagues showed in 1970 in an important paper in the *British Journal of Social and Clinical Psychology*, if an unfriendly message is delivered in a friendly tone of voice, with a smile, its hostile contents are discounted and the message is thought to be friendly.

Moral for meetings: don't soften bad news – its recipients will merely misunderstand you.

Californian kinesic researcher Albert Mehrabian, in two series of experiments which he reported in 1967, established that people are influenced far more by the tone of voice and facial expression of the speaker than by the words used.

On the basis of his work, Mehrabian postulated the following equation:
Perceived attitude $= 0.07$ (words) $+ 0.38$ (tone) $+ 0.55$ (face)

Or, less mathematically, the facial expressions of a speaker are almost eight times as powerful as the words used.

Somewhat less dramatically, a more recent study by Argyle showed that non-verbal signals have about four and a half times the effect of verbal ones.

And, although the words 'body language' suggest corporeal posture to be the critical factor in non-verbal communication, every scrap of experimental data shows the face – especially the eyes and voice – to be key.

On average, in conversation we look at each other for about one third of the time.

To look less often, or to look away determinedly, conveys boredom and lack of interest; to look a *little* more often conveys enthusiasm and attraction; to stare continuously almost always causes embarrassment. Dominance can quickly be established by 'staring the other person down'.

Dominant apes do much the same: another feather in Darwin's cap.

Dominance is established more forcibly still by tone of voice and vocal expression.

Dominance is directly correlated with loudness and with perceived confidence.

(Once again, science confirms traditional wisdom: 'He who shouts loudest usually gets his own way.')

Low-pitched voices are more dominant, high-pitched voices more submissive.

A varied pitch suggests that its owner is dynamic, pleasant and happy, presumably too dynamic and happy to worry about his uncertain oscillations between dominance and submissiveness.

We all know that a wealth of feeling can be communicated by facial expressions. It is therefore hardly necessary to follow Professor Ray Birdwhistell through his labyrinthine analysis of eyebrow positions (4), eyelid positions (4), mouth positions (7), and so on.

We simply need to remind ourselves that a deftly timed quizzical glance, a disbelieving raise of the eyebrows, a sceptical crinkling of the forehead, can unsettle even the most voluble Talkie in full flood.

Do not, though, push your thespian talents too far; you are neither Marlon Brando nor Sarah Bernhardt.

As Dr Albert Scheflen has warned, kinesics do not provide a how-to-do-it manual 'on seduction, salesmanship or gaining popularity'.

Rather, kinesics provide hints and clues to the unconscious motives and emotions of others.

This is particularly true of bodily – other than facial – movements and postures.

Here are some common body-language mannerisms, with their translations:

* we rub our noses in puzzlement
* we cover our eyes with our hands to reject information we find distasteful
* similarly, many of us move our index fingers across our nostrils – we really do, just watch – if we disapprove of what we're hearing
* alternatively, for the same reason, we pick insignificant specks of dust from our clothes
* we hold our noses to display disdain
* we cuddle our own arms to isolate and protect ourselves
* to display indifference we shrug our shoulders, to display impatience we tap our fingers
* most useful of all, meeting-wise, most of us cover our mouths when we are unsure of what we are saying, particularly when we are lying; if the man's mumbling, it is probably because he's fibbing.

(Our psyches, it seems, are a lot more honest than we are.)

Demonstrations of mental aggression are frequently
displayed as symbolized gestures of physical aggression:
clenched fists, table banging, punching the air, leaning
forward.

When you lean forward, you threaten to invade other
people's space.

Humans, like other animals, psychologically own the
personal space surrounding them.

The study of this sub-category of kinesics is called
proxemics, and has been led by Dr Edward T. Hall,
Professor of Anthropology at Northwestern University.

Dr Hall has divided the space in which each of us operates
into four zones: (i) intimate distance, (ii) personal
distance, (iii) social distance, and (iv) public distance.

Intimate distance, from nil to eighteen inches, may be
comfortably entered only by our spouses, lovers, children
and close family; friends and other relatives are allowed
into our personal distance, from eighteen inches to four
feet; social relationships, which typically occur in
meetings, fall between four and nine feet.

It is easy to demonstrate, and many experiments have
done so, how easy it is to disturb people by trespassing in
their personal space. Even moving your personal property
– a bag or a cigarette pack – into other people's space may
well distract them.

Consciously or unconsciously, aggressors frequently
invade others' territory to establish dominance.

While most meetings are seated, space invasions can be
deployed effectively before the event begins or, though
obviously less significantly, after the show is over.

Once seated, however, you should relax, for two reasons.

First, because Goffman (1961) and Mehrabian (1968) have separately shown that higher-status people sit casually or even slump in meetings, while their inferiors perch anxiously upright.

Second, and more important, because the ever-watching Birdwhistell in his tome *An Introduction to Kinesics* showed that leaders don't fidget.

Too much body movement conveys – who would have guessed it? – uncertainty and immaturity.

Finally, every book on non-verbal communication stresses the importance of clothing.

As with all other aspects of body language, plumage is primitively but inescapably influential.

Nowadays meetings, and fashions, come in so many shapes and styles that it is impossible to proffer detailed rules on how you should or should not dress.

The only sound advice is to dress differently but not – unless you are as certain of your brilliance as Disraeli or Wilde – outrageously.

Dress to impress.

Which brings us to our Fifth Law of Meetings, a law which summarizes the entire contents of this chapter in six, for most of us depressing, little words.

As far as meetings are concerned: **you are what you look like.**

7

In the Chair

Innumerable words of advice have been written to help chairmen chair.

These range from Robert's legalistic *Rules of Order*, through the Institute of Directors' *Standard Boardroom Practice* and on to the Playboy Press's *How to Make Meetings Work*.

(Let's eschew the neologism 'chairperson'. The *Oxford Dictionary* definition of chairman – 'the person chosen to preside over a meeting' – is felicitously asexual.)

If you become reasonably proficient, being chairman is one of the most entertaining, exhilarating and enjoyable roles at a meeting.

Cynics would claim it to be the *only* entertaining, exhilarating and enjoyable role at most meetings.

The power and responsibilities of a chairman are enshrined in British law (though not a lot of people know that):

> 'It is the duty of the chairman, and his function, to preserve order and to take care that the proceedings are conducted in a proper manner, and that the sense of the

meeting is properly ascertained with regard to any
question which is properly before the meeting.'
                (*National Dwellings Society* v. *Sykes*, 1894.)

For a century or so, more time and effort have been
devoted to investigating, analysing and defining
chairmanship than to any other aspect of meeting activity.

Despite which, the 1960 *Harvard Business Review* survey
of management executives' opinions stated that the great
majority believe 'the problem is not so much committees
in management as it is the management of committees'.

From which it is easy to deduce the Sixth Law of
Meetings: **the perfect chairman does not exist**. Proof: it is
a rare meeting which ends without at least some, and
often most, of the participants grumbling irascibly about
the way the chairman has handled at least some, and often
most, of the issues. This is the inevitable result of the
chairman's two inherently contradictory responsibilities:

* to ensure fair play
* to force the meeting along and, occasionally, reach
  decisions.

All the existing research agrees that to resolve this
dilemma the chairman must be, and must be seen to be,
firmly and positively in charge – without being bullying or
over-assertive.

A tricky tightrope to tread.

Shlesinger, Jackson and Butman, for example, showed in
a series of experiments reported in the *Journal of Social
and Abnormal Psychology* (1960) that individuals who
were seen to exert greater control were rated more skilful

as chairmen, and as more valuable contributors to a committee's work.

Likewise, L. Berkowitz in his important study *Sharing Leadership in Small Decision-Making Groups* (1953), showed that 'leadership sharing' was related inversely both to participant satisfaction and to eventual output.

Yet it is crucial for the chairman not to interfere too much; particularly if the chairman, as so often, coincidentally happens to be the boss.

E.P. Torrance found that high-status participants in meetings are extra-successful in getting their ideas accepted: even when they are wrong.

Or, as a German businessman I met once said, jokingly (I think), 'My subordinates tell me I never make a mistake.'

Barry Maude reports in *Managing Meetings* (1975) that the National Industrial Conference Board discovered the most common pitfalls in meetings to be caused by chairman dominance, especially when (a) the chairman talks too much himself; (b) the chairman inhibits free discussion by leading questions and offering suggestions; and (c) the chairman keeps the meeting going too fast and fails to provide enough time for the group to develop its own solutions.

Consider, in contrast, this statement by John de Butts, the then chairman of American Telephone and Telegraph:

'In meetings I try to be sure that everybody has an opportunity to speak. I'll ask questions so that people who haven't spoken will have the opportunity to say something . . . When it gets to the point where we seem to have reached a consensus I might say, "Well let me

try and sum up and see if this is where we are.''
Sometimes somebody doesn't agree, and then we have
to talk a bit longer. Then I'll try to sum up again. But a
successful meeting depends on how much everybody
participates, not on how long it goes on.'

(Quoted in *Harvard Business Review*,
January/February 1974)

In a world of imperfect chairmanship, that is a fine
statement of the principles involved in being a perfect
chairman.

However, it neatly sidesteps the problems; and the
problems, of course, are people – of whom, if you are
chairman, the most exasperating quartet are:

The whisperers, who chatter and giggle with their
neighbours and must be ruthlessly silenced before they
irritate everybody else.

The loudmouths, a mongrel sub-species of Talkie, who
need to be muzzled sympathetically, since if they are
gagged too quickly they may (a) become obstreperous,
and (b) possibly win the sympathy of the meeting, for
having been cheated of their democratic right to speak.
(Let them go on too long, however, and the meeting gets
fed up with both them *and* you.)

The interrupters, another sub-species of Talkie – and
often a boss who hasn't got to be chairman – they need
continually to be restrained from continually butting in
on everyone else, lest meeting strangulation takes place.

The cracked records, usually Passionates, who keep
repeating the same point over and over, even when the
meeting has moved on to entirely another subject, and
who must be gently but firmly reminded that their views

have already been considered and noted – and that further repetition will drive everyone raving mad.

One time-honoured way for a deft chairman to fetter such folk is to catch their eye infrequently.

They must be allowed to chirp sometimes, or they will eventually sing out with a legitimate grouse; but, if they receive just marginally fewer than their fair share of speaking opportunities nobody – except maybe them – will notice.

Another nimble way to control speakers, used very effectively by the Right Honourable Shirley Williams MP when she is chairing large meetings, is to nominate five or six speakers at a time, selecting the speakers who need to be restrained to speak first:

'First you Joan, then Harold, then Charles, Belinda after that and finally William.'

This neatly forces the earlier speakers to be a trifle more succinct than they might otherwise have been, under pressure from the others itching for their turn; and, if perchance one of them does maunder on, the chairman can interrupt and remind them of the queue still waiting.

Every textbook on meetings lists the duties of chairmanship: make clear the terms of reference, define the objectives, ensure that speakers keep to the agenda, and so on.

Moreover, social psychologists' findings have generally confirmed the traditional textbooks' wisdom. N.R.F. Maier, for example, in 1953 hypothesized a number of leadership skills necessary for the management of meetings and then obtained experimental evidence of their value. These were:

* identify the problem, consider the available facts, and ask each member of the group for his views about the important factors
* make sure minority views are expressed, as this leads to more accurate solutions
* focus on disagreements in the group and try to arrive at creative solutions
* evaluate different solutions in relation to criteria if these can be agreed upon
* ask stimulating questions to make the group question its approach and consider other aspects
* divide problems into sub-problems which can be taken in turn.

Additionally, L.R. Hoffman in his 1965 paper *Group problem-solving* showed it to be advantageous always to make meetings consider two possible solutions to any problem – since the second usually proves superior to the first.

All unexceptionable, all fairly obvious.

However, a recently devised meeting management method called the Interaction Method has been invented by Michael Doyle and David Strauss and is detailed both in their popular Playboy Press book *How to Make Meetings Work* (1976) and in their follow-up documentary film, based on the book.

The Interaction Method as described by Doyle and

Strauss re-allocates the usual responsibilities of the officers in formal committees, and gives the new officers hyped-up new titles:

- The Chairman does not run the meeting.
- The Facilitator does run the meeting, but doesn't express opinions.
- The Recorder records the Group Memory, in other words takes Minutes.
- The Participators are the *hoi polloi* who, as always, do the work.

From our present point of view, the most interesting function is that of the Facilitator, who is expected to take over most of the responsibilities of the traditional chairman, without enjoying titular control, viz:

'The Facilitator –
   Is a neutral servant of the group
   Does not evaluate or contribute ideas
   Focuses group energy on common tasks
   Suggests alternative methods and procedures
   Protects individuals and their ideas from attack
   Encourages participation
   Helps the group find winning solutions
   Co-ordinates pre- and post-meeting logistics.'

Which is not, when you study it, so different a definition of the chairman's role from that of the old judge in *National Dwellings Society* v. *Sykes* way back in 1894.

Thus the fundamental principles of chairmanship have changed less than radically over the years.

Except in one aspect: body language.

As Doyle and Strauss, and all other recent commentators, have emphasized, the chairman is better able to exploit body language than any other meeting participant.

Many researches have shown that most members of a meeting consistently keep their eyes on the chairman.

The chairman must therefore be hyper-aware of his posture (erect, positive, dominant) and of his facial expressions (lively, interested, encouraging).

If you want to be a chairman, say goodbye to the drooping eyelid and occasional post-prandial doze.

Excruciating though it may sometimes be, you'll have to stay alert.

It's the price you have to pay for the entertainment, enjoyment and exhilaration.

Possibly it is the unwillingness of many meeting-goers to sacrifice their snoozes which explains why most small meetings don't have chairmen at all.

Yet they swing along well enough without them.

8

The Law

More than sixty historic court cases have been concerned with the conduct and consequences of meetings.

They range from *Garden Gully Quartz Mining Company* v. *McLister* (1875), which established that decisions reached at board meetings by persons acting invalidly as directors are not binding on the company, to the Gordon Hotels case (1956), which established beyond further legal dispute that an adjourned meeting is merely a continuation of the original meeting.

(It's jolly reassuring to have such self-evident truths confirmed by the judiciary.)

For commercial and business meetings, the most significant statutory instruments are the Companies Acts of 1948 and 1976.

And you'll find the best brief precis of all the legal folderols in Hall's *Meetings: Their Law and Practice*, which calls itself a handbook yet runs to over two hundred pages.

We earlier defined, and will continue to define, a meeting as comprising three to about twenty people, but in law

(*Sharp* v. *Dawes*, 1876) a meeting is 'the coming together of at least two persons for any lawful purpose'.

Indeed, and despite the above decision, the law whimsically allows that in certain circumstances a single person can constitute a valid quorum (*East* v. *Bennett Brothers*, 1911).

A judicious ruling, which many meeting-goers would like to see enforced more frequently (and was doubtless in Herbert V. Prochnow's mind when he first formulated his famous rule – see page 6).

The first simplistic rule about meeting law is: don't break it. Like Al Capone being caught for tax evasion, many operators have tripped themselves up by being caught meeting-cheating – pretending to have held meetings that did not happen; fudging the minutes; holding a legally required meeting in a legally invalid way.

To hold a legally valid meeting, the gathering must be:

Properly convened, with every person entitled to attend having been invited and given sufficient notice.

Properly constituted, it being the duty of the chairman to ensure that the prescribed quorum is present.

Properly held, in accordance with any regulations governing the conduct and procedure of the meeting.

The regulations governing a meeting should define how its officials are to be appointed; the chairman's powers, and particularly the contentious question of whether or not he has a casting vote (see *Nell* v. *Longbottom*, 1894); how the quorum is to be convened; the order of business; voting and proxies; and the form of acceptable motions or resolutions, amendments and debate.

Perhaps most important of all, the regulations must specify precisely when and how the regulations themselves can be altered.

(The laws of human nature demand that there will always be disgruntled players who try to move the goalposts when they fail to score.)

Of course, all of these statutory hijinks primarily refer to formalized committees, rather than to informal get-togethers.

The great majority of meetings are not convened: they're chucked together; they have no structure: they meander haphazardly; they boast no chairman – the most senior person present struggles valiantly to keep some semblance of order.

Nonetheless, you must never forget that verbal agreements, no matter how lightly entered into, may well be contractual and legally binding.

Especially if, as is generally the case in meetings, there are witnesses.

All successful meeting manipulators are closet barrack-room lawyers.

At political, institutional or company meetings they will point out points of order and infringements of procedure faster than you can say 'objection overruled'.

So long as it's to their benefit.

There is probably no top businessman in the world who has not yanked procedural law, by the scruff of its neck, into a committee or board meeting.

Even in the most casual encounters, it is possible to
deploy quasi-legal rulings advantageously:

> 'That's totally outside our terms of reference.' (Even
> when no terms of reference have been agreed.)

Or, aggressively:

> 'That's completely out of order, and you know it.'

Despite all of which, immodesty compels me to claim
that, in matters relating to our subject, the laws of the
courts are far less important than the Laws of Meetings.

Of which the Seventh states that in meetings, as in life: **the
law's an ass, but don't horse around with it.**

*   *   *

Not even a lawyer could consider meeting law to be the
most scintillatingly stimulating of subjects, so let's break
for a well-deserved adjournment and enliven the tedium
with some frivolous meeting games.

After which, in chapter 10, we'll return refreshed and
suitably earnest to investigate a type of meeting that is
truly no laughing matter: the brainstorming session.

9

Games Meeting-people Play

As we noted earlier, and despite conventional clichés to the contrary, meetings are not games.

This need not stop you playing games in meetings.

Noughts and Crosses, Boxes, Hangman and other classroom contests have saved the sanity of many a meeting-goer during protracted procedural wrangles and points of order.

More serious skirmishes with which to while away interminable, intricate and irrelevant investigations include Battleships, Pegoty-on-Paper, various forms of sophisticated Dot-to-Dot, and even Memory Chess if you're clever enough and can find a partner.

Gladiatorial jousts of this kind are of course played merely to pass the time – unlike the strategic games we'll be describing later, which are deployed to attain victories and trounce enemies.

Half the fun of playing is that doing so is just as naughty as it was at school, and must likewise be well hidden from the teacher, alias chairman.

Extreme naughtiness comprises talking in class and

under-the-breath mickey-taking, forcing those nearby to choke back giggles as best they can.

Like at school.

Most such games must be played by two or more.

For loners, reading books and magazines under the table (desk) are old favourites, as are crosswords.

Patricia Mann, a vice-president of the J. Walter Thompson advertising agency and an almost professional meeting-goer, passes happy hours scrambling the names of all those present into apt anagrams. (She turned Winston Fletcher into SH! WENT FOR CLIENT – a perfect adman's anagram.)

Another good game for loners, invented I believe by Chris Wilkins, creative director of the Young & Rubicam agency, is called Euphemize the Minutes.

To play, you merely write the minutes of the proceedings, during the proceedings, in your head, in the way that you would prefer the outside world, or anyway your superiors, to read them:

> 'The negotiations didn't go quite as expected.' (It was like Dunkirk . . . without the boats.)

My own solitary first choice I've dubbed Freud 'n' Fraud.

To play, you will just need a pencil, paper and a schoolboy sense of humour.

Play consists of listening closely to everyone's oratory – this is an incidental advantage, since most other games take one's ears, so to speak, off the ball – and jotting

down both the accidental *doubles entendres* and the all-
too-deliberate pomposities.

They can either be listed in two columns on either side of
a page or underneath each other like inconsequential
speeches in a surrealist drama.

It increases the fun if you add your own dramatist's
comments as you go.

Here, for example, without amendment, are the Freud 'n'
Fraud notes I took at a directors' meeting of one of the
country's leading dry-cleaning companies. In most cases,
you must remember, the speaker was responding to
somebody else's remark, which makes sense of his own;
but making sense of the conversation isn't part of the
game.

'It's far too rigid.'

'Do you think we could do anything on eiderdowns?'

'We'll achieve penetration in November.'

'Let's look at the bottom then.'

'No. It's going to be long and hard.'

'The identification of independent variables
masquerading as something else is a real lump with
which we must treat.' (*What? Ed.*)

'It's just a row of large holes.'

'And surely our next period started yesterday?'

'I need a bigger one.'

'The action plan is how.' (*Appears to reveal a glimpse of
Red Indian ancestry. Ed.*)

'It's got to be chopped off.' (Managing director, hysterically.)

You get the gist. A subtle mind is not required.

Another small ball of fun worth bowling occasionally is Chinese Whispers.

Leaning to your neighbour you mutter, 'Don't want to raise this one myself, but could you ask Jim to ask Eddie to question why . . . mumble, mumble.'

Don't aim to get your question passed too far – people just aren't that amenable – and make sure its unwitting final destination is a Talkie; Passionates and Seers rarely co-operate.

Even when you've set everything up perfectly, four times out of five it fails, but just occasionally the trick works a treat, justifying all your efforts and making meeting life truly worthwhile.

The very best game of all to play on your own, however, depends upon your being the most senior person present.

(Even a most junior person is a most senior person sometimes.)

It's no good if you're chairman; indeed, if the meeting has a proper chairman, the game cannot be played at all.

It has no name, but could be called Too Bad, I'm Boss.

As boss, your *droit de seigneur* entitles you to be (a) completely silent, and/or (b) waywardly inconsistent.

You can sit through the entire proceedings like a Mum, never uttering, while your silence gets louder and louder and everyone gets edgier and edgier.

This is beautifully consummated by an early departure.

Stand up, say nothing, turn at the door, say, 'Thank you everyone,' smile enigmatically and vanish.

It is probably the only occasion in life when it is entirely certain that the party will really warm up after you've left.

If you don't feel like acting dumb Mum, the alternative way to enjoy Too Bad, I'm Boss is to twist, turn and reverse the flow of the proceedings unpredictably, like an inebriated caller at a barn dance.

Thus, if the participants have been convened to investigate urgently ways to reduce production costs, you cheerfully but forcefully suggest that, instead, they should be considering ways to increase costs and charge higher prices.

Or, if the problem under discussion is faulty telecommunications, you ask naively but repeatedly whether the root cause of the difficulty isn't personnel management . . .

(Played deftly, such diversions will not only create chaotic confusion, but will simultaneously enhance your reputation as a profound and lateral thinker.)

Again, when you have set up the chaos, an early departure will not come amiss; don't make it too early though – leaving eight to ten minutes before the final whistle is due to be blown is perfect.

Our last game for loners demands a collaborator, but one who isn't in the meeting.

It is also a game which can be played for serious purposes, as you'll see in the Sprint, page 172.

It's called Sorry, It's Urgent and involves you being summoned from the room to deal with a crisis at a time when your presence is veritably crucial.

This requires a little prior planning and guestimating, but it can often be achieved.

While you are absent, the meeting idles like an engine in a traffic jam, and frequently stalls.

Sometimes this will help you win a worthwhile meeting victory on your return; at the very least, it will provide you with a harmless chuckle as you sit in your office, feet on the desk, reading *Private Eye* or *Playboy*.

Well, games for one are fun but games for more are better.

A couple of splendid tedium alleviators for two or more are Drag the Word In and Inventaproverb.

Drag the Word In is the easier.

Before the meeting, or secretively during its course, each player gives the other an unlikely word to bring naturally into the discussion.

The first person to use his designated word is the winner.

(If you predict an exceptionally long and tedious assembly, you can play with three words, or even five; but trying to incorporate more than five becomes, in my experience, hideously complicated.)

Words which seem promising often turn out not to be.

Elephant, for example, is a surprisingly simple word to drag by the tusk into business debates:

'With the launch of this new widget we'll charge like an elephant through the jungle of the competition.'

Or, less acceptably (unless, that is, it's really a good idea!):

'What about giving away a free plastic elephant with every case of our new widgets?'

Drag the Word In shouldn't be played as a kind of variant of Call My Bluff; there is no point in giving your competitors words they've never heard of, like broggle, or gowk, or lophodont – tempting though it may be.

Asparagus is a good word, unless the meeting is likely to last till lunchtime – so are blowpipe, dairy, marmalade, raffia and turmeric.

There are only two rules. First, every word chosen must be in a nominated dictionary acceptable to all players.

(It's probably the only one in the building, the one belonging to the MD's secretary, with pages 407–19 missing.)

Second, words must be used relevantly and not shouted as sudden expletives, e.g., 'Marmalade, dammit!' or 'Turmeric to you, you sonofabitch!'

Applying this rule inevitably calls for fine judgement, and Drag the Word In can therefore be played only by Gentlemen of Honour, employing mutual trust and confidence.

Of which there is, as everyone knows, no surplus in meetings.

Hence Inventaproverb, which is an advanced variation of Drag the Word In, is yet more difficult to play.

Inventaproverb was itself invented, legend has it, by Jeremy Bullmore, chairman of J. Walter Thompson. (Admen seem, predictably enough, to be fertile inventors of meeting games.) Like Drag the Word In, it is usually played by two, but any number can join in.

The first task is to invent a phrase which sounds like an authentic proverb, an adage tried and trusted and true – which seems pregnant with philosophic subtlety, but in fact has no meaning whatsoever beyond its face value.

The words must mean just what they say, and as little as possible; not a profound jot nor sapient tittle more.

Jeremy Bullmore's two old favourites are:

> 'Somebody has to bury the undertaker.'
> 'It may not be the man who saws the logs who needs the fire.'

Those I like include:

> 'The face that laughs is also the face that cries.'
> 'A little rain can only make you wet.'

'You don't need to look through the glass of an open window.'

'Leaves on the ground have fallen from the trees.'

And best of all, meetings-wise:

'Success is merely failure in reverse.' (Or indeed, vice versa.)

Care must be taken to avoid phrases which might, just might, have a deeper meaning.

Phrases like:

'You can't cross the road without crossing the gutter.'

'Only a young doctor has never lost a patient.'

'Only a foolish watchmaker is deaf to the music of time.'

Or even:

'The fastest car on the road is the one which passes the rest.'

To return to the game. Once the meaningless proverbs have been invented and agreed, they must be used in the meeting just as in Drag the Word In.

They must be delivered sententiously, even pompously, and must appear to be relevant and thoughtful contributions to the subject under discussion.

The first player thus to use his proverb wins.

If anyone in the room shows even the merest awareness that something a trifle odd has been said, the player is deemed disqualified.

Finally, a few words about doodling.

Rare is the regular meeting-goer who doesn't doodle.

Occasionally, by scavenging around after important political and international meetings, journalists scoop up great men's doodles and publicly analyse their meaning in the press.

A deplorable habit which, in our more modest way, most of us have tried from time to time: deciphering meaningless scribbles, gazing blankly at jottings as if they were tea-leaves.

Well, according to leading graphologists, we, and the journalists, are wasting our time.

(Unless, that is, we discover written notes instead of mere doodles.)

Doodles – graphologists and psychologists generally agree – reveal little more than handwriting itself does.

That is, they expose deep-seated obsessions and personality traits, rather than instant feelings and reactions.

So, if you spy people doodling, it's worth watching out for:

* those drawing rectangles: wider bases reveal thoughtful planners; while smaller bases with wide tops reveal gamblers, optimists likely to build castles in the air and make bricks without straw

* framing: doodles in which a frame is an organic and essential part indicate orderliness and clarity of mind –

people whose doodles are disorganized are, surprise, surprise, likely to be disorganized themselves

* whether the doodler leaves his sketch alone and keeps starting afresh or goes on altering and adding; the latter is a perfectionist, the former a dilettante

* musical notes, weapons, sexual symbols, etc., require no profound interpretation; they show the doodler to be absorbingly interested in music, fighting, sex, etc

* lastly, and again predictably, repetitive patterns disclose a lack of imagination, arcs and strokes reveal uncertainty, while arrows tell of frustration

If you notice two people doodling together, they're probably playing Noughts and Crosses.

In which case it is kindest to leave them be.

Such kindness is anyway often rewarded when the players remain too absorbed to notice a point you want to win, and to which they are implacably imposed.

On the other hand, if you believe they'll support you, interrupt immediately.

For the Eighth cruel Law of Meetings states that: **those who play games in meetings must learn to suffer spoilsports.**

10

Brainstorming Sessions

We now move from mindless games to games of the mind: brainstorming sessions.

Brainstormers should, strictly speaking, be outside the scope of this book; but it hardly seems possible – in this day and age and at this moment in time – to ignore their existence entirely.

Brainstormings should be outside our scope because, as defined by leading enthusiast J. Geoffrey Rawlinson, they are:

'A means of getting a large number of ideas from a group of people in a short time.'

Rawlinson himself claims to have generated over 1200 ideas for a chicken-food manufacturer in a 3¾ hour session – which my pocket Panasonic makes 5.3 ideas per minute or one idea every 11.3 breathless seconds without stopping for nearly four hours.

An awesome strike rate, which nonetheless ranks tardily behind the latest *Guinness Book of Records* attempt, in which ten Manchester managers sprinted 280 ideas for improving the British economy in just 480 seconds: that's one per 1.7 seconds.

(The previous Guinness record was established by a US Navy group in 1961, but they managed a mere 210 ideas in the time.)

All of these extraordinary statistics spotlight one of the reasons why brainstorming is of little interest to us here.

Nobody can manipulate a meeting in which ideas are being zapped out like machine-gun fire.

Since they were invented by adman Alex F. Osborn in the 1930s, and popularized by Osborn and Sidney J. Parnes in the 1950s, brainstorming sessions have happily gone out of fashion.

(Though in the 1980s they appear to be enjoying a slight swing-of-the-pendulum resurgence.)

The reasons for the decline in popularity may, again, largely be deduced from the absurd Olympic statistics quoted above.

Throwing up incoherent, undisciplined ideas truly isn't difficult.

But problems, and particularly costs, derive from the time and effort necessary to analyse and evaluate their feasibility.

Imagine the poor, harassed chicken-food manufacturer faced with 1200 mostly nutty (I almost said *fowl*) ideas.

Even if he could immediately strike a thick red magic-marker through 1150 of them – and doubtless he could – that still left fifty in need of further investigation.

Fifty ideas, almost by definition impossible to rank for priority, and all of them bastards.

Without a parent, that is.

We all know what becomes of ideas without parents: particularly ideas that are radically new and difficult to effect.

They get lost in the filing system; they get accidentally omitted from minutes; they get left till the end of meetings and postponed; and postponed; and postponed again, until they pass forlorn and forgotten to the great idea graveyard in the sky.

I have attended innumerable brainstorming sessions – with their free-wheeling, don't-you-dare-criticize, don't-hold-back-we-promise-we-won't-laugh-at-you rules.

Some were stone cold sober, others well hooched.

Some have been tediously dreary, others hilarious fun.

Nothing worthwhile has ever resulted from any of them; not a single, itsy-bitsy usable idea.

My own experiences have been confirmed by the professional psychologists.

To quote Professor Michael Argyle in *The Social Psychology of Work*:

'When brainstorming sessions have been compared with individuals they have usually been found to be inferior. Individuals are better at generating ideas –

group discussion is more useful for evaluating ideas than for thinking of them.'

Nothing that's been said above should be taken to imply that meetings can never be creative and can never solve problems.

They can and do.

But brainstorming sessions?

Whether they're Synectic Groups, or use the Kepner-Tregoe Method, or the introspective Gendlin Focus Method, or the Guiden Imagery System, the best thing you can do is keep well away.

That's the Ninth Law of Meetings: **the only rule you need to remember about brainstorming sessions is avoid them.**

If you've any good ideas, you'll need to fight for them like a tiger.

If you've no good ideas, don't kid yourself that sitting in a room with a dozen or so equally uncreative folk will turn you into Shakespeare or Leonardo or Newton or Einstein.

It won't.

You'd be far better off looking for a nice, old-fashioned meeting to manipulate.

11

Everything's Negotiable

'Sex apart, negotiation is the most common and problematic involvement of one person with another, and the two activities are not unrelated.'
(Professor John Kenneth Galbraith)

We're warming up and working our way towards the 21 key stratagems with which you can gain the maximum mileage from meeting manipulation.

Our last staging post *en route* is negotiation.

Many of the skills and strategies necessary in negotiation are the same as those used in meetings generally.

Or in life generally.

Personal conflict is a growth industry.

To quote the first line of Herb Cohen's American bestseller *You Can Negotiate Anything*:

'Your real world is a giant negotiating table, and like it or not, you're a participant.'

Or as he later adds, in apt if less than pretty prose:

'What is negotiation? It is the use of information and

power to affect behavior within a "web of tension". If you think about this broad definition, you'll realize that you do, in fact, negotiate all the time both on your job and in your personal life.'

Correction, Mr Cohen.

For most of us, the innocent truth is that we do not view our real world as a giant negotiating table, nor do we negotiate all the time either in our jobs or in our personal lives.

Naturally, this leaves us prey to those who do.

However, with thought, effort and practice, even the most guileless of us can transfigure our negotiating performance.

Then at least we cease to be sitting ducks.

(Though it may still be advantageous to look as if we are.)

Significantly, Herb Cohen devotes little of his book to the pre-planning of negotiations.

His off-the-cuff approach is typically American, a by-product of the belief that all of life is negotiable.

(Even the most energetic must find pre-planning their entire life somewhat arduous.)

In predictable contrast, every German book on negotiation devotes much of itself to detailed planning and analysis.

German negotiators decide precisely what they want beforehand and calculate precisely how to get it.

This characteristic inflexibility by no means always works to their advantage; often, they miss tricks which the more flexible, pragmatic and exuberant American approach would have won.

And while we are on the subject of national negotiating stereotypes it is worth noting a few more:

* the French prefer to keep negotiations to broad principle, and especially, like De Gaulle, enjoy saying 'No'

* to Middle Easterners, time is far less important than it is to Westerners; they are greatly concerned with trust, and they will extend the early, exploratory phases of any important negotiation indefinitely, so that all concerned can get to know each other socially – nor are they fazed by interruptions and delays; on the contrary, they revel in them

* Mediterraneans and Africans tend to accept 'lubrication' as normal in negotiations, since the giving of gifts to those with whom one is dealing is traditional behaviour

* Japanese negotiators care deeply about status – they feel uncomfortable dealing with people of either much higher or much lower rank; and they rely greatly upon expert advisors, which doubtless explains why they are in this respect like the Chinese, so concerned with 'face'.

This incidentally spotlights the first key rule of negotiation: you will always do better for yourself if you provide your adversary with a deal which he finds agreeably acceptable; or, at the very least, which he can portray as acceptable to colleagues and superiors.

In other words, as the victors learned so expensively after the First World War, don't screw losers too hard.

Westerners, as much as Easterners, hate losing face.

Which brings us to the British style of negotiation.

The British are seen by everyone else to be

- amateur
- under-prepared
- flexible and responsive
- kindly and agreeable.

The quintessential image of the British abroad; and an image burnished by British diplomats and the Foreign Office.

Well, as we've hinted – and this is doubtless the Foreign Office point of view – in negotiation it does no harm to be underestimated by your adversary.

Provided that you finally prove your adversary wrong.

Disregarding cultural differences, in any negotiation three of life's fundamental forces will be present.

No, not faith, hope and charity.

(Certainly not charity.)

Knowledge, time and power.

Knowledge: the other side invariably seems to be better informed about you and your needs than you are about them and theirs.

Time: the other side never seems to be under the same time constraints and restrictive deadlines as you.

Power: the other side always appears to enjoy more power and authority than you.

We'll investigate each in turn, starting with knowledge.

All knowledgeable negotiators know knowledge to be the heart of the matter.

Why then do so many of us so often enter negotiation inadequately informed?

Partly because we're busy, partly because we're idle, and partly because we think we're so quick on our feet we can shoot from the hip off the top of our heads.

Result: we are felled by fusillades of facts.

All possibly relevant facts are important – watch a canny barrister in court – but the most crucial of all is to know in advance your when-all-the-chips-are-down end-play.

Exactly what, in other words, happens if both sides are immovably intransigent and refuse to budge a microjot.

Too many negotiators are naive optimists.

They enter the ring smiling cheerfully, confident that their opponent will be reasonable, that there will be a bit of give and take, and that after a little ritual table-banging a sensible compromise will be reached.

Sometimes it is. Sometimes it isn't.

Either way, you will take more and give less, and the

compromise will be less compromising, if you are certain of your final fallback position from the start.

This is called by Roger Fisher and William Ury, respectively director and associate director of the Harvard Negotiation Project, your BATNA: your Best Alternative to a Negotiated Agreement.

Fisher and Ury, probably the most experienced negotiation researchers in the world, place a great deal of importance upon the BATNA.

'The better your BATNA, the greater your power,' they claim, and they continue:

> 'Vigorous exploration of what you will do if you do not reach agreement can greatly strengthen your hand. Attractive alternatives are not just sitting there waiting for you; you usually have to develop them. Generating possible BATNAs requires three distinct operations: (1) inventing a list of actions you might conceivably take if no agreement is reached; (2) improving some of the more promising ideas and converting them into practical options; and (3) selecting, tentatively, the one option that seems best.'

To start developing BATNAs before negotiations begin sometimes seems unduly pessimistic.

On the contrary.

In negotiations, buoyant optimism is almost always asinine.

'It is a great nuisance,' wrote W. Somerset Maugham, 'that knowledge can only be acquired by hard work.'

Nuisance or not, knowledge is power.

(Incidentally, that's a seventeenth-century proverb, not a dazzling twentieth-century discovery.)

Let's now move our finger on to time.

Time is not to be confused with timing.

Time, as we shall see, is something you can control, whereas timing – though unquestionably crucial in negotiation – is an instinct which, as we have said before, regrettably cannot be learned.

Most people enter a negotiation thinking of it as an event with a fixed beginning and end (often, and deliberately dramatically, dubbed the 'deadline').

Whereas one of the key rules of negotiation is that deadlines, like rules, are made to be broken.

The negotiator who decides first that he doesn't give a doodle for the deadline is in a marvellously advantageous position.

Keep in mind that deadlines are almost always more flexible than they appear; evaluate the gains and losses that will accrue if you go beyond the brink; remember that the other side, cool and serene though they may look, have a deadline too – and that their seeming tranquillity may well mask ulcerous stresses and pressures.

During one of the largest and most lucrative negotiations in which I have ever been involved – the sale of an office block – I regularly shifted back the deadline after it had been set, each time finally and immutably, by the other side.

Each postponement caused the confused purchaser to increase his bid until the eventual price paid was some eight times his paltry opening offer.

Never reveal your own final, shatterproof deadline.

Above all, always act as if you have all the time in the world: this will irritate and unnerve your adversary into making mistakes and giving ground.

Which is the object of the exercise.

Having considered knowledge and time, let us turn to power.

In negotiation, power is largely based upon perception; so, if you think you've got it, you've got it.

Any oaf can negotiate from strength; the only dexterity necessary, as we've noted, is to avoid overplaying your hand.

True artistry is to win from weakness.

In negotiation, however feeble your position you are never, never ever, entirely powerless.

Here, then, are thirteen lucky ways to help you build, and more importantly flex, your negotiating muscles even when you enter the fray feeling like a seven-stone weakling:

Invade their territory: contrary to conventional wisdom, it is almost always advantageous to meet on the other side's turf; they will feel more important, be more relaxed, thus be more susceptible to your wiles – and, if they aren't, it will be easier for you to walk out.

Open the bidding: this advice, for which I am indebted to the late Douglas Collins, founder of Goya and self-made millionaire, enables you to control and determine the tone and scale of the discussions – if you begin by demanding a million pounds, your opponent will feel silly responding with an offer of a few thousand; it is, of course, a tactic commonly used by trades unions when wage bargaining.

Pick a nit: even the tiniest nit can, like a hole in a dyke, provide a worthwhile breach in your opponent's argument; when you are buying something, look for any itsy-bitsy blemish which, like a pimple, can be inflamed with a deft scratch.

'Whatif?': 'whatif' is a magic phrase in negotiation; 'whatif I buy two?', 'whatif I agree to pay cash?', 'whatif I sign a three-year contract?'

(NB: 'whatif?' is far more effective as a promise than a threat. E.g., 'whatif I decide not to go ahead?' will probably achieve little, whereas 'whatif I go ahead without further delay?' will probably spark a reciprocal offer that can be exploited.)

Make 'em compete: there are always other fish in the sea, other pebbles on the beach, other girls in the world; in negotiations, as in romances, a well-timed wink from the green-eyed monster will work wonders.

Hang on in there: in negotiation, most people quit too quickly: plodding, pig-headed perseverance prevails.

Give a little, take a lot: always carry into negotiation a few worthless trinkets that you can willingly give away, and watch out for others that you can painlessly concede as the joust proceeds.

Sweet talk: everyone knows flattery won't get you everything, but it will help you negotiate an awful lot, (though note Carnegie's Crunchers on page 109).

Sweet listening: inexperienced negotiators often consider it clever not to give the other side's case any serious attention, and not to admit any legitimacy in their point of view; experienced negotiators do just the reverse.

Take a gamble: good negotiators, like good poker players, bluff and gamble only rarely and cautiously; but they do bluff and gamble – it's part of the art.

What a larf!: American second-hand car dealers are taught to burst out laughing as soon as a car is presented to them for purchase; such belittling giggling can unsettle even the most confident adversary.

Help, help: in negotiation, dumb is often better than smart, inarticulate frequently better than articulate; and weakness can be strength, since only bullies enjoy kicking people when they're down.
(NB: It is, needless to add, vital to watch out for bullies.)

Invest their time: the more time a person invests in a negotiation, the more willing he will be to reach a compromise rather than see his efforts totally wasted; this is another key rule when you are negotiating from a feeble position – a sizeable investment of your adversary's time will often pay vast dividends.

Having discussed tactics, we must now assess style.

There are truly only two negotiating styles: aggression and conciliation. The very first two of the Seven Deadly Skills.

(The conciliatory style is sometimes subdivided in

textbooks into two – collaborative and compromise. Deeper investigation proves these two styles to be, in practice, inextricably intertwined.)

Roger Fisher and William Ury have defined the two styles thus:

Conciliatory	**Aggressive**
Participants are friends	Participants are adversaries
The goal is agreement	The goal is victory
Make concessions to cultivate the relationship	Demand concessions as a condition of the relationship
Be soft on the people and the problem	Be hard on the problem and the people
Trust others	Distrust others
Change your position easily	Dig into your position
Make offers	Make threats
Disclose your bottom line	Mislead as to your bottom line
Accept one-sided losses to reach agreement	Demand one-sided gains as the price of agreement
Search for the single answer: the one they will accept	Search for the single answer: the one you will accept
Insist on agreement	Insist on your position
Try to avoid a contest of will	Try to win a contest of will
Yield to pressure	Apply pressure

Which style you employ will depend both upon your personality and upon whether the negotiation is to be a single, once-and-for-all event or is part of a continuous relationship.

Herb Cohen, like most negotiation pundits, claims that you can afford to risk being more aggressive in single-occasion negotiations than in continuing associations.

My own experience is the reverse.

People are nicer, and need to be nicer, to people they hardly know than to people they know well.

If you are unpleasant to a stranger, you will probably provoke an aggressive reaction.

In negotiation, this is unlikely to be beneficial to you.

If you are unpleasant to a colleague or friend, you may well intimidate, or at least depress, them.

Unquestionably, many successful negotiators rant and rave ferociously, and daily, at those with whom they deal; and as often as not they win respect for their over-zealous dedication.

The aggressive style of negotiation – or Russian style as it is sometimes called – can be awesomely effective.

Unfortunately, it is all but unlearnable.

If you are the kind of person who screams and shouts, you find it easy; if you aren't, you probably can't.

Don't be dismayed though.

Although it sometimes seems otherwise, especially in the short run, there is no evidence to show that the noisiest negotiators always triumph.

A fine example is the most famous Russian temper tantrum in post-1945 history: Khrushchev's temperamental shoe-pounding at the United Nations in New York in 1960.

Thumping the UN lectern with his boot heel provided plentiful psychological pleasure.

History does not suggest, however, that he scored many points by his performance.

In negotiation, as in all competitive activities, naked aggression occasionally pays off, but is just as often counter-productive.

Remember Don Corleone's wise words in *The Godfather*: 'Never get angry. Never make a threat. Reason with people.'

A few words about ultimatums.

Ultimatums are usually best avoided.

They inevitably irritate your adversary, and define limits and deadlines which fetter your own freedom.

Very occasionally, however, they are a useful tactic:

* when you know, but the other party does not, that the passing of time is disadvantageous to your position

* to force a speedy yes or no when you have the opportunity to follow an alternative course of action if the negotiation fails

* when the other party is congenitally indecisive.

Do not be misled, however, into believing that once you've issued an ultimatum you must stick by it, come hell or high water.

Few people do.

(Listen to parents threatening their children with dire and dreadful consequences which never come to pass.)

It's bad behaviour.

But nobody has ever suggested that negotiation brings out mankind's most admirable and endearing virtues.

Lastly, often the very best advice about negotiation is: don't.

Find somebody else to do it for you.

Preferably somebody who is more expert in the subject than you, or may be a better negotiator than you.

Above all, somebody who will need to refer to you for their final authority; this will give them tremendous advantages in the negotiation.

Alternatively, if you cannot find someone suitable to be a stand-in, pretend to be a stand-in yourself.

Invent an implacable, hard-hearted higher authority whose agreement you will need before a concordat can be reached.

This is a ploy I often play.

You may find it a trifle painful to your pride.

Console yourself with the thought that, if it results in a glorious victory, that's a paltry price to pay.

PART TWO:

The 21 Key Stratagems for Success

We have at last reached the moment when you can begin to manipulate meetings in earnest.

Here are 21 key stratagems with which to outplay, outclass and outmanoeuvre your fellow meeting-goers.

A stratagem, according to the *Oxford English Dictionary*, is:

'An artifice or trick designed to outwit or surprise the enemy; a device or scheme for obtaining an advantage.'

Few of the 21 stratagems, therefore, are ploys or gambits, move-by-move manoeuvres of the kind employed in Chess or American football.

Meetings are usually too variable (that's a euphemism for chaotic) to allow you to adopt predetermined gameplans.

As we said earlier, to succeed you need to combine forethought and planning with nifty reactions once the joust is in progress.

The 21 stratagems will help you cope successfully with most eventualities.

However, that is not a claim that the compilation is exhaustive; it certainly is not, never could be.

New stratagems are being invented incessantly, hour by hour and minute by minute, somewhere at one of the world's 50 million daily meetings.

So that our Tenth and final Law of Meetings must firmly state: **even the world's most Machiavellian meeting manipulator can be outplayed, outclassed and outmanoeuvred by a greenhorn with genius and guile.**

That's what makes meetings such fun. (Such *what*?)

1

Blow Up

Our first small stratagem is designed to demolish ideas
and schemes which you dislike.

It is particularly popular in the entertainments industry,
where it is sometimes called Let's Make it a Ballet, or
sometimes simply Wagner.

As with most destructive stratagems (except for Full
Frontal), your initial reaction to the scheme you intend to
pulverize must be to greet it with Deadly Skill number
three, enthusiasm (page 27).

With such effusive enthusiasm, indeed, that you wonder
whether the originator may not have been much too
modest in his plans?

Surely so strong and original an idea is worthy of a far
greater investment of time and resources? Surely
everyone has sufficient faith in it to forge ahead without
further research? Surely it could be the basis for a truly
major enterprise?

Surely it would make a stunning ballet?

The proud parent will be so encouraged that he will
zealously support his infant's inflation.

After all, how can he possibly know whether you are being genuinely enthusiastic or just playing Blow Up?

As the stratagem develops, it is vital to prod others into support for the cause.

Otherwise, your own role may, as matters progress, seem somewhat inexplicable.

For, as soon as you judge that the bubble has been blown up as big as it will go without bursting, you must take one of two courses of action.

The first, and safest, is to begin to puncture it there and then.

If the idea has been pumped up quickly and thoughtlessly, this will not be difficult.

'It's certainly an amazingly, astonishingly, fantastically, wonderful scheme, but . . .' is the key phrase.

At which point the negative thinkers, idea crushers and party-poopers who populate every meeting will plunge in with rapidity and relish.

Plus, of course, anyone with a personal grudge or vendetta against the originator.

Should any of the critics drag their feet, you can spur them into action:

> 'I still think the whole conception is spellbinding, but you have a worry or two don't you, John?'

John always has a worry or two, or three or four.

By now, the original little scheme will be forgotten, or at best seem boring and pointless.

Even its author will have lost interest; it will be almost impossible to resurrect.

The second, and riskier, course of action is not to undermine the blown-up project but to propose that it be deferred for further exploration.

This has several advantages.

First, it completely guarantees that the original idea will not be reconsidered.

Second, everybody leaves the meeting feeling expansive and cheerful.

Third, much time may then be devoted to investigating the scheme, while you can concentrate on important issues more likely to reach fruition.

(In my experience, though, this third advantage often fails to take effect, since after a good Blow Up most of the participants awaken the next morning realizing that in the heat of the meeting the project got out of hand and became a bit silly.)

Despite these putative advantages (which many Blow Up players swear by), my personal view is that it is unwise to risk leaving the project undemolished at the end of the meeting.

Its protagonists, if they are skilful, may manage to progress it without reference to future meetings, and thus without further hindrance.

Go for sudden death is my advice.

That way, whenever you successfully Blow Up the idea you'll successfully blow up the idea.

2

Blushers

Professor Erving Goffman, guru of face-to-face behaviour, demonstrated in his classic work *The Presentation of Self in Everyday Life* that all social behaviour involves a great deal of deliberate deception.

(Anybody who spends much time in meetings quickly reaches the same conclusion; you don't need to be a professor.)

Embarrassment, Goffman goes on, is caused when the bogus image is discreditied.

Indeed, in one thousand instances of embarrassment collected by sociologists E. Gross and G.P. Stone (*American Journal of Sociology*, 1964), about one third of the cases involved the unmasking of deliberate deception.

A second way to cause embarrassment is rule-breaking.

H. Garfinkel showed in a series of demonstrations in 1963 that, when his investigators behaved abnormally – treating other customers in shops as salesmen, behaving like lodgers in their own homes, and so on – those involved became embarrassed and frequently failed to cope with the situation.

All researches have shown, hardly surprisingly, that embarrassment doubles and redoubles when it occurs in front of groups: the greater the number present, the greater the embarrassment.

Which is perfect for meetings.

Because those embarrassed lose poise, lose concentration, blush, stutter, fumble, sweat, avoid eye-contact and, on occasion, even flee from the room.

So that Blushers is a stratagem that can sometimes win you outright victory instantaneously.

Here then are ten ways to embarrass antagonizers, some mild, others more obnoxious:

* consistently address people by the wrong name; even after you have been put right, continue to do so, apologizing as you correct yourself

* remembering Gross and Stone, publicly discredit any bogus image (such as your opponent's credentials), if you possibly can; do so without gleeful and malicious overt enthusiasm, but do so

* employ disdainful phrases like 'my dear boy', 'of course that's a fairly common point of view', 'surely what you are trying to say is ...?', 'I don't think you really understand at all ...', 'I don't think you really meant to say that, did you?'

* invent relationships that do not exist: refer enthusiastically to a stranger as 'my close friend', declare your admiration for individuals you despise, your fond affection for individuals you can hardly tolerate

* query persistently why action has not yet been taken,

even (indeed especially) if there is no reason why the
action should have been taken

* point out any oddities in people's appearances and
personal habits; it sounds childish but 'do you *really* like
that tie you're wearing?', or 'do stop fidgeting' or 'had a
rough night last night, did you?', let alone 'do you
always pick your nose like that?' are all omnipotently
destructive

* conversely, if you have the confidence to dress
unsuitably, then you will disconcert at least the more
conservative of those present, so that they may well be
unable to cope with you at all

* try a Garfinkel and act subserviently, even cravenly
towards people subordinate to you; so strongly imbued
are our views of hierarchy that most people find such
behaviour torturously embarrassing

* ignore obvious hints, when others make convoluted
suggestions which affect you but which they do not have
the courage to state outright; better still, deliberately
misunderstand; often the hinter will be embarrassed
into dropping the point entirely

* grab at offers and invitations clearly intended for
others, even if you later neglect them yourself.

As you can see, embarrassing others in meetings calls for
little skill, yet can bring rich rewards.

Two final words of warning.

First, as with all stratagems, never forget that the ploys
you play on others can also be played on you.

Thicken your skin, grit your teeth, and refuse to be
embarrassed or to let embarrassment unsettle you.

Second, do not go far too far.

Goffman and Gross and Stone (above) have separately shown that, when a person is publicly put in a predicament, others present may try to help, since embarrassment is curiously contagious and the embarrassment of a person itself causes embarrassment to those around.

So, when you play Blushers, you must cautiously follow the wise advice of that old shaving-cream advertisement: not too little, not too much, but just right.

3

Boredoom

US President Jimmy Carter was, by any standards, an exceptionally steadfast, decent and ethical fellow.

He was also one of the most boring leaders in the world's history.

(An unkind commentator once quipped, 'When Carter gave a Fireside Chat, the fires went out.')

Fortunately, he knew his own strengths, or rather weaknesses, and sometimes used them to advantage.

As in the Camp David negotiations between Egypt's President Anwar Sadat and Israel's Menachem Begin.

Camp David will never be a watering hole for the playboys of the western world. It has been said that the most exciting thing to do there is sniff pine cones.

During the negotiations, Carter provided just two bicycles for the fourteen people present, plus a choice of three movies as evening entertainment.

By the sixth night, everyone had seen the films twice and was bored brainless.

And each day at 8.00 a.m. Jimmy tapped on Sadat's and Begin's cabin doors to hurry them back to the negotiating table.

By day thirteen, Sadat and Begin would have signed almost anything to escape the tedium.

Carter had bored them into submission.

The same stratagem can be employed, to bring doom as well as gloom to others, in many meetings.

Most of us are so conditioned to avoid being boring that we find it all but impossible to bore intentionally.

Moreover, most meetings are so soporific that to encourage you needlessly to add to their torpor would be wickedly and unforgivably immoral.

So don't do it too often.

Not that it is easy to bore purposefully. As Hilaire Belloc put it:

> 'For *deliberate* and *intentional* boring you must have a man of some ability to practise it well, as you must to practise any art well.'
>
> (*A Guide to Boring*)

Boredoom can reduce the most vigorous opponent to placid stupefaction.

It will sap the most passionate of Passionates' vitality.

Allowing the bore to win a walkover. (Or even a sleepwalkover.)

If you are normally a fascinating and amusing speaker –
and of course you are – how can you turn yourself into an
irksome bore, at will as it were?

The best hint is to think of anyone you know well who
bores effortlessly and mimic them.

(While it is hard to emulate the Wildely witty, it is
distressingly easy for most of us to imitate bores; perhaps
we're not as fascinating and amusing as we think.)

Be repetitive; talk quickly; don't modulate your voice;
include appalling jokes; laugh at them; sound a little nasal
if you can; don't pause or speak in sentences; don't look
at anyone else; stare at your hands; don't worry about
being illogical or incoherent; above all, ignore
interruptions and drone on interminably until you are
literally compelled to stop.

Do everything, in fact, that you normally make
gargantuan efforts to avoid doing.

Once you get going, it is truly monstrous fun.

Occasionally, I blast the odd Boredoom at particularly
persistent salesmen.

It reduces them to awestruck stupefaction.

I once heard a brilliant Boredoomer sell a sizeable sales
consultancy contract to a critical committee,
approximately thus:

   'We all talk about increasing sales don't we, I mean
   when it comes to sales we all like to talk about them
   going up, increasing really, getting much more and so

on, don't we, but when we think about sales there are
three things I want to say, just three things but they're
all important, really important although there are only
three of them and the first is this, the very first, not that
they are in any order of importance really, well as I was
saying the first is that it's all very well for us to sit up
here talking but it's the chaps out in the field, the chaps
taking the orders, the reps, the poor old rep, he's the
one at the sharp end and it's too easy to forget that, we
all forget the old rep but he's the one we rely on, really,
without him we're nowhere are we, have you ever
thought of that? because he's the one that really
matters, him or her I mean because I know of course
you've one of two members of, um, shall we say the um
gentle sex, not that some of yours are all that gentle, ho
ho if you don't mind my saying so . . .'

By the time he reached his third point which, like his
second, proved to bear an uncanny resemblance to his
first ('I can't emphasize enough how much we depend, I
mean really rely on, the chaps, and not forgetting the gals
of course, let's never forget the gals, ho ho, the ones at
the sharp end I mean . . .) his audience would willingly,
like Sadat and Begin, have signed almost anything to
silence him.

Let us finally repeat that Boredoom is a stratagem to be
used infrequently.

Partly out of kindness to others.

Partly because too much practice might make you just too
perfect; and the doom you're boring for may prove to be
your own.

4

Carnegie Crunchers

Although its cloying charm is out of fashion, Dale Carnegie's six-million-copies classic *How to Win Friends and Influence People* is not all bad news.

Carnegie was a meetings man to the core.

Reading his double-plus bumper bestseller, you get the impression that he hardly existed at all when he was alone, so enthusiastic is he about warm and loving human relationships.

Many of his tricks and techniques are now so well known that they have become conventional wisdom, the accepted dogma of social intercourse:

'Be a good listener. Encourage others to talk about themselves.'

'Remember that a man's name is to him the sweetest and most important sound in the English language.'

'Try honestly to see things from the other person's point of view.'

'Begin in a friendly way.'

'Let the other man do a great deal of the talking.'

'Talk about your own mistakes before criticizing other people's.'

'Talk in terms of the other man's interests.'

All sound, if somewhat simplistic, meeting precepts.

(It's incidentally interesting to note Carnegie's unselfconscious male chauvinism, which was apparently unexceptionable in 1938 but would be wholly unacceptable today.)

Some of Carnegie's stratagems are well worth exploring in more depth.

First: **You can't win an argument**.

Not quite an eternal truth, but a useful rule-of-thumb.

As Carnegie says:

'You can't win an argument because if you lose it, you lose it; and if you win it, you lose it.'

The Germans have a word for this: *totsiegen* (winning yourself to death).

Or, as Benjamin Franklin put it:

'If you argue and wrangle and contradict, you may achieve a victory sometimes; but it will be an empty victory because you will never get your opponent's goodwill.'

Clearly this advice is more applicable to debates *à deux*

than to sizeable meetings, where it is usually impossible to win your case without forceful argument.

Nonetheless, the underlying principle applies: be wary of those you trounce – they'll be waiting for any opportunity to achieve sweet revenge.

Second Carnegie: **Get people to say 'Yes, Yes.'**

Socrates beat Carnegie to this particular perception by about twenty-three centuries.

(And the Chinese probably got there a couple of thousand years still earlier, when they aphorized, 'He who treads softly goes far.')

The Socratic method of philosophic dispute is built upon asking questions with which one's opponent cannot disagree.

Socrates would win one admission after another until eventually, without always realizing it, his opponent found himself embracing an argument he would bitterly have dismissed a little while earlier.

Skilful and successful salesmen use exactly the same psychologically sound technique.

As Professor Overstreet states in *Influencing Human Behaviour*:

'A "No" response is a most difficult handicap to overcome. When a person has said "No", all his pride of personality demands that he remain consistent with himself. He may later feel that the "No" was ill-advised; nevertheless there is his precious pride to consider!

Hence it is of the very greatest importance that we start a person in the affirmative direction.'

As true for meetings as it is for metaphysics.

Third Carnegie: **Smile**.

This has become such dog-eared advice that you may feel insulted at its mention.

Every shop assistant's lapel badge and every junk-shop mirror cries out 'Smile'.

Carnegie, again, did not say it first.

Another historic Chinese proverb says, 'A man without a smiling face should not open a shop!'

So it's not just old hat, it's veritably ancient.

However, a book on meetings which did not remind its readers to smile would be culpably negligent.

Every bit of psychological research on the subject shows that you're more likely to put across a case convincingly if you do it with a smile.

Go on, as Carnegie advises, *practise*; it doesn't hurt.

Fourth and final Carnegie: **Make other people feel important – and do it sincerely!**

Before you puke, hold on a second.

Carnegie is more subtle than at first he seems.

As psychology's founding father William James claimed, 'The deepest principle in human nature is the craving to be appreciated.'

Carnegie seems to have based his entire view of humanity on that single precept.

He would not have been an adept Blushers player.

He states that Confucius, Lao-Tse and Buddha all promulgated different versions of one and the same belief, and:

> 'Jesus summed it up in one thought – probably the most important rule in the world: "Do unto others as you would have others do unto you."'

(Wrong, Dale C., Jesus didn't say it. It's a fourteenth-century proverb.)

For Carnegie, this advice would mean rapidly spotting the admirable qualities – physical or mental – of everyone in a meeting, and complimenting them on those qualities as soon as possible.

Like it or not, that's How to Win Friends and Influence People.

Carnegie went further.

His rule, remember, added 'do it sincerely' to the initial 'Make other people feel important'.

The word 'sincerely' has been debased since Bernie Cornfeld's less-than-totally-scrupulous IOS insurance salesmen were trained to open every sales pitch with: 'Do you sincerely want to be rich?'

Then Lord Olivier did the word little good when he quipped, in answer to a question about the secret of success, 'Sincerity. Sincerity. Once you can fake that you can achieve anything.'

Carnegie's point is less cynical.

He deplores crude flattery, insisting that it is transparent – and so is true sincerity.

Well, personally, I'm with Lord Olivier.

However, it is not my intention to quibble with Carnegie.

His ideas are folksy, and corny, and sentimental.

None of which makes them wrong.

So stop sneering. Which meetings do you attend that are so desperately sophisticated and subtle?

5

Cheesecake

Cheesecake photography reveals little, but hints at lots: its aim is stimulation by titillation of the imagination.

In this permissive era, cheesecake has, sadly, gone the way of all flesh.

Except, happily, in meetings.

Cheesecake is, as you will later learn, the full-frontal opposite of the Full Frontal.

It works by hints and innuendos, by inferences and allusions.

It is sometimes called Insider, which hints exactly at its nature.

This, for example, was a fine Cheesecake stratagem played against me by a fellow who, with his partner, was trying to inveigle me into selling my advertising agency.

FELLOW: 'One's always hearing rumours of course. I take no notice of them.'

PARTNER: 'Too true. Although there's no smoke without fire, they say.'

WF: 'What are you both going on about?'

FELLOW (*laughing*): 'It's like when your wife's having an affair. The husband's always the last to know.'

PARTNER: 'Nobody wants to tell him.'

WF: 'I still don't know – '

FELLOW (*interrupting*): 'It's your clients, bonehead. We're talking about your clients.'

WF: 'Clients?'

PARTNER: 'Well, no names no pack drill, they say.'

WF (*getting riled*): 'I still – '

PARTNER: 'Your clients. That's what we're talking about. Your clients.'

FELLOW: 'And the fact that four of them, I happen to know from private sources, are looking around. At other agencies. At the moment.'

WF (*after lengthy pause*): 'Which four?'

FELLOW: 'Maybe more for all I know.'

WF (*moving from riled to rattled*): 'Rubbish.'

PARTNER: 'I wish I had your confidence. I really wish I did.'

WF: 'Crap. Which of my clients are you talking about?'

FELLOW *and* PARTNER *exchange glances:* 'Love to tell you, but we really can't. Honestly.'

Needless to say, they resolutely refused to reveal the names of the clients who they claimed were looking around. In trying to shake my confidence in my business, their purpose was obvious; and I didn't believe them (I still tell myself).

Nor, however, could I totally disbelieve them.

They kept me guessing, unsettling me, provoking me to lurch between defence and attack.

The inevitable results of a skilful Cheesecake stratagem.

As it happens, on that occasion they lost – they were a smidgen too greedy.

They also went on a little too long, which transformed my uncertainty into irritable anger.

That's a vital caveat about Cheesecake: it irritates so effectively that it must not be overplayed.

However, several of their lines were perfect Cheesecake cues:

'I never believe rumours of course, but . . . '

'There's no smoke without fire.'

'I happen to know from private sources.'

'I wish I had your confidence.'

'I'd love to tell you, but really can't. Honestly.'

And here are half a dozen more which often come in handy:

'I know my customers.'

'Maybe I shouldn't have, but I've been speaking to some people in your department.'

'I've been shown a confidential document.'

'Are you sure you've told us everything?'

'It was before you joined the company.'

'People's private affairs are their own business.'

By definition, non-verbal signals are ideal communicators of innuendo and allusion.

Quizzically raised eyebrows, stares of shock and horror, winces of astonishment and disbelief will all enhance your Cheesecake repertoire.

Getting back to the verbals, never clarify or elucidate; successful Cheesecakes are built upon brevity.

So that Talkies tend to play poorly.

However, with training and self-discipline even the most garrulous can learn to play adequately.

I'd love to tell you how, of course, but I really can't. Honestly.

6

Fight the Wrong Fight

Fight the Wrong Fight is like throwing a feint, but better.

When you feint a punch (or a pass), you throw the opposition off course by pretending to throw the punch (or the ball).

When you Fight the Wrong Fight, you both throw the opposition off course and throw the punch.

You choose an unimportant issue about which you care little and use it as a decoy to deliver arguments that relate to an important issue about which you care lots.

You must, if necessary, manipulate the agenda to ensure that the unimportant issue is raised first; it's rather late to throw a feint after you've lost the fight.

Fight the Wrong Fight is like diversionary attack on the battlefield, but again better.

It provides seven benefits:

* you will be able to deliver your arguments twice
* using the unimportant issue as a trial run enables you to

tease out the strengths and weaknesses of your opponent's case

* likewise, you obtain advance warning of who your enemies and supporters will be in the later battle

* you can start to wear down, and possibly even wear out, the opposition

* you can minimize the time available for discussion of the more important issue

* you may be able to avoid dissension, bad feeling and spleen adhering to the major issue, if most of it has been vented previously (this, when applicable, can be an immense benefit)

* by boxing cleverly, you can either (a) win the minor issue, which the opposition may not be bothered to fight for fiercely, and then use the victory as logical proof of the soundness of your arguments, or (b) deliberately lose the minor issue to win the major one as a *quid pro quo*.

(If that sounds like heads-I-win-tails-you-lose, it is.)

Fight the Wrong Fight is especially useful in any meeting where you are putting forward a series of alternative ideas or solutions to a problem.

If, say, you are putting forward several possible computer programmes to a customer, then you should include, early on, a programme similar to the one you intend finally to recommend, and fight for it like a tiger.

Some people fear that a defeat of the decoy proposal may make it impossible to force through the real one.

Not so – not unless the real one was anyway beyond salvation.

As the decoy is being demolished, you must be rehearsing in your mind the reasons why your later proposals completely overcome all the difficulties being raised.

That is precisely the point and purpose of Fighting the Wrong Fight.

(Incidentally, it is desirable to distance the two Fights as widely as possible, both so that you have time to rehearse between them, and to avoid repeating yourself like a cracked record.)

The only real risk you run when you Fight the Wrong Fight is of winning the wrong fight and losing the right one.

Even the best laid plans, of mice and men, in meetings gang a'gley.

7

Frighteners

Despite Don Corleone's cynical advice to the contrary (page 91), Frighteners can be marvellously effective meeting manipulators.

As long as you handle them adroitly.

The broad principles were outlined under aggression, the first of the Seven Deadly Skills.

Here we'll delve into more detail.

The effectiveness of a Frightener manifestly depends upon the fear or anxiety it arouses.

Psychologists differentiate between fear and anxiety: fear has an identifiable cause, anxiety does not.

Fear can be seen and recognized; anxiety lurks in the shadows.

Thus 'If you go ahead you'll be fired' will provoke fear; whereas 'If you go ahead there'll be some pretty unpleasant consequences' will provoke anxiety.

Almost always, as we emphasized when discussing aggression, it is wiser to provoke anxiety than fear.

(As unscrupulous politicians have always been well aware.)

Psychological researches have also established that surprise exaggerates both anxiety and fear.

In meetings this means that, if you intend to arouse a little anxiety, give no prior indication of your intentions: play your cards tight against your chest.

Unsurprisingly, many psychologists (see, for example, P.G. Zimbardo, E.B. Ebbeson and C. Maslach, *Influencing Attitudes and Changing Behavior*, 1977) have shown that people in a state of anxiety are far more influenceable than others.

Which is what meeting manipulation is about.

(And doubtless explains, in passing, why most brainwashing techniques are anxiety-based.)

It is risky to aim Frighteners collectively, at everyone present.

For, as Elton T. Reeves showed in *The Dynamics of Group Behavior*, groups (as against individuals) are usually strengthened in their cohesion and resolve when threatened.

As often happens in war.

So the three rules we've developed for Frighteners run:

* keep them nebulous
* keep them up your sleeve
* keep them divisive.

It will now be apparent why the classic Hollywood clichés recommended earlier (page 24) fit the bill perfectly.

(High-class Hollywood scriptwriters have always been high-class psychologists.)

From the psychological point of view, then, the more nebulous threats are the better.

From your own point of view, the more nebulous threats are the simpler they are to invent.

It is easier to warn people that in certain circumstances they will suffer dark and dire consequences if you need not specify either the circumstances or the consequences.

As if you were in Hollywood, you'll need a little menace in your voice, but otherwise don't overdramatize:

'You're going to regret this, you know.'

'Do you really understand what the outcome will be?'

'You'd better think very carefully about that.'

Naturally, those threatened will respond with a 'Why?' or a 'What do you mean?'

Be unswervingly enigmatic.

Of course in the real circumstances of a real meeting you should be capable of inventing better Frighteners than those listed.

Equally nebulous, but more relevant.

A gentle way to play Frighteners, strongly recommended by Harvard's Roger Fisher and William Ury, is to eschew threats and substitute warnings.

Fisher and Ury claim that threats generate counter-threats (which has not been my own experience in meetings); whereas warnings are less provocative.

Specific threats can sometimes be better phrased as warnings. To return to our earlier example: 'If you go ahead I can only warn you that you'll be fired' will often be preferable to the bolder 'If you go ahead you'll get fired'.

However, the nebulous threatening Frightener is still best.

Finally, the finest Frighteners of all are frequently self-immolatory.

Such as Egypt's Nasser and France's De Gaulle threatening to resign their respective countries' leaderships in order to regain power with still greater authority than before.

As with withdrawal, the last of the Seven Deadly Skills, serious self-immolatory Frighteners must be used sparingly.

If you repeatedly threaten to resign, some day someone will accept.

Lesser threatened self-punishments, however, are safe and strong:

'I'll pay for that with my own money if it fails.' (You'll never be asked to.)

'I'll work through my vacation to get it done, if I have to.' (If you do have to, you'll be able to claim the time back later, probably with interest.)

'I'll take a cut in salary to pay for my secretary, if that's the only way to keep her.' (Nobody ever takes a cut in salary, but it's a hard threat to overrule.)

Tossing Frighteners around adroitly is not that difficult.

If you can't handle them, you'd better stop going to meetings before you . . .

8

Full Frontal

There are occasions when subtlety and deviousness are as irrelevant as last week's agenda.

Occasions when the right way to tackle the situation is full-frontally, head-on.

To help you recognize such occasions, the best guidance that can be given is both negative and obvious: never attack full-frontally unless you know you can win.

Don't full-frontal your boss.

It may just be acceptable, if he is an exceptionally amicable fellow, for you to do so in private – between consenting adults, so to speak – but not in public at a meeting.

In meetings, boss manipulation must be more circumspect.

Cogitate carefully before full-frontalling Passionates or Seers.

The former will lose their temper and you will risk losing control of the situation; the latter will ride the punches and make you look silly.

Unless being paid to do so professionally, no sensible person ever enters a fight, or a war, unless he knows he will win.

(Though fools do it all the time.)

When Fabius led the Roman army into battle against Hannibal, he avoided a full-frontal confrontation because he knew he would be routed.

Instead, he developed his famous Fabian guerrilla tactics: keeping to the hills, avoiding battle, harassing Hannibal at every turn.

After six months, Fabius's appointment as general expired, and he was replaced by two generals, each of whom controlled the army on alternate days.

(How on earth did the Romans build a great empire with daft ideas like that?)

One of the two was a rash, battle-eager muttonhead.

On his day in charge, he marched the army out to meet Hannibal full-frontally.

Of the 76,000 Romans sent onto the battlefield, 70,000 remained there for ever.

To repeat: never attack full-frontally unless you know you can win.

If you tend to suffer, like the Roman general, from incurable I-can-lick-'em-all optimism, then you must force yourself to be extra cautious and fetter your aggression with iron restraint.

In meetings the key to winning full-frontal frays is
assertiveness.

Leading management consultants Ken and Kate Back
suggest in their book *Assertiveness At Work: A Practical
Guide to Handling Awkward Situations* that assertiveness
can solve almost all of life's little problems.

Which assertion perhaps goes a little too far.

In their devotion to assertiveness, Ken and Kate come out
aggressively against aggression; whereas aggression is
listed in chapter 5 as indubitably one of the Seven Deadly
Skills.

The difference is partly definitional, partly real.

On the definitional side, non-physical aggression – which
is what we are here talking about – can often be described
as mere assertiveness.

On the other hand, in meetings, forceful but controlled
aggression (*instrumental* aggression) often wins the day.

As the Backs put it:

> 'The aim of aggression is to win, if necessary at the
> expense of others.'

Right on, Ken and Kate, right on.

The matter has been worth belabouring because, as a
meeting manoeuvre, the Full Frontal depends upon
assertiveness rather than aggression.

Which will be good news to those who are unaggressive by
nature and instinct.

The essential ingredients for a successful Full Frontal are:

Be brief: it is all but impossible to be assertive if you meander and maunder on. (You may think the loquacity of great orators proves otherwise but (a) orators have captive audiences whereas you don't, and (b) without wishing to denigrate your talents unfairly, the likelihood of your being a great orator is less than minuscule.)

Ride roughshod over interruptions, even from the chairman should there be one: you cannot be forceful and assertive while simultaneously being sensible and co-operative.

Attack ideas rather than individuals: the particular dangers of attacking Passionates and Seers have already been mentioned; but the advice is more general, if not always applicable – remember that the Full Frontal is assertive rather than aggressive.

Time your Full Frontal carefully: the gambit is almost always better employed earlier, pre-emptively, rather than later when others have dug themselves into immovable positions.

Use assertive body language: tone of voice is especially important; don't get shrill but speak loudly, dominantly, confidently, and stare people down while you are speaking. Ration your rhetorical gestures, but a sudden, out-of-the-blue table thump may add a nicely noisy touch of emphasis.

The great historian of military strategy and tactics B.H. Liddell Hart concluded from his studies that full-frontal attacks in war are both futile and a horrible waste of manpower.

Successful leaders, he claimed, outmanoeuvre and outflank their opponents, as Fabius did.

This is generally true of meetings, too – as the very existence of this book implies.

Nonetheless, my own belief is that Full Frontals could and should be used more often than they are.

Most of us are far too nice in meetings.

A little aggro is a splendid thing.

9

Hassle the Chairman

Perhaps because he is a figure of authority, it is often possible to Hassle the Chairman more relentlessly than other meeting members.

(In meetings without chairmen it is sometimes possible to achieve the same results by hassling one or two senior people present.)

It's especially easy if the chairman is easygoing, inexperienced, lax, or too anxious to be democratic.

Precisely the characteristics of those schoolmasters who, you remember, were unable to keep discipline.

What is the purpose of the stratagem?

If you are sufficiently successful, you become the chairman manqué; while the true chairman becomes your ventriloquist's dummy.

You can pressure the meeting, via the chairman, to skim rapidly over some items and debate others at length.

You can influence the chairman's choice of speakers, urge him to interrupt some and encourage others.

You can persuade him to take a vote, or to refuse one.

It is far better to achieve all this, if you can, without being the proper chairman – since the chairman must be fair, and open-minded, and unprejudiced, and responsible, whereas the hassler need suffer no petty constraints.

To play Hassle the Chairman effectively, you must get going immediately the meeting begins.

Pick on a point of order with which you can criticize the chairman's handling of the proceedings right at the start.

If the chairman tries to 'take the minutes of the last meeting as read', complain that it isn't acceptable; if he doesn't, complain of the waste of time.

Almost invariably and inevitably the chairman will commit insignificant gaffes which can be lambasted; if he doesn't, invent them.

By now, the chairman is getting unsettled and keeping a wary eye on his tormentor.

To no avail.

Arriving at an agenda item which you do not wish to have discussed, look exaggeratedly at your watch and demand that no time be wasted on so unimportant an issue.

Then complain loudly that the chairman has consistently devoted far too long to trivial matters and rushed through the important ones.

At the very least, this diversion will destroy serious

discussion of the particular agenda item which has by then been reached.

Having taken a few moments' breath, return to the fray to play Red Herrings (page 161) with totally minor, footling issues, demanding furiously that they should not lightly be dismissed 'just because the chairman wasted time earlier on totally minor, footling issues'.

A grand master of Hassle the Chairman is Oliver Stutchbury, one-time managing director of the huge Save and Prosper Group of Unit Trusts and now a politician extraordinary.

On one occasion, halfway through a meeting, I well remember Stutchbury stating:

> 'There can be no point whatsoever in continuing to remain in this meeting if the chairman is determined to force us into debating paltry trivia at interminable length, and is equally determined to refuse us sufficient opportunity to discuss matters of crucial substance.'

I remember it well because I was the chairman.

After so imperious a statement, the chairman is likely to be in a cold sweat. (I was.)

Effectively, Stutchbury had control of the meeting.

Whether or not the others present approve of what is happening hardly matters; for the hassler, it is another heads-I-win-tails-you-lose situation.

If the others argue, the meeting moves towards chaos, from which it can only be recovered when the hassler chooses to relax; if they stay Mum, the hassler wins by default.

Hassle the Chairman is a stratagem that should only be undertaken if your personality is up to it.

You must relish a hassle.

If you do, you may even be able to improve upon Stutchbury's parting quip at the previously mentioned gathering.

Becoming aware of the stratagem being played against me, I sped the agenda through its final stages – and particularly rapidly through an item I suspected Stutchbury wished to discuss.

As we closed, he turned to the others and said sweetly:

'May I move that we minute our congratulations to the chairman for finishing the meeting early. For the first time ever.'

10

I'll Write a Document

'Never volunteer' is an old army maxim which doesn't apply in meetings.

(It is difficult to think of two human institutions less similar than meetings and the army: the former revolve around discussion, consensus, equality and indecision; while the latter is built upon commands, obedience, hierarchy and decisiveness. Meetings in the army are doubtless quick, but they can't be much fun – unless you're the senior officer present.)

Even in meetings, however, you must volunteer only occasionally, in very particular circumstances.

The other old motto 'If you want a job done ask a busy man' is absolutely true; but you don't want it to apply to you, do you?

The most rewarding voluntary work to undertake is document writing.

I'll Write a Document is a development of the well-known meeting phenomenon: he who writes the minutes controls the decisions.

(Summing up verbally at the conclusion of the

proceedings – whether you have been invited to or not – is a less arduous substitute for minute-writing, but not nearly so effective.)

The minute-writer has power because few people will bother to read the minutes anyway; even fewer will be bothered to correct them if they are wrong; and even those who do so can usually be convinced they have misremembered what occurred, as likely as not because they were in the land of nod at the time.

For similar reasons, volunteering to write a document is a masterful way of taking control of an issue.

It sounds conscientious; it sounds generous; it sounds sensible; it whisks the matter out of the hands of your opponents; it allows everyone else to stop worrying by simultaneously pandering to their self-importance ('We've delegated it to him') and to their idleness ('Of course, we'll check the document carefully in due course').

Maybe they will, probably they won't.

Get your timing right and you should be able to clear the document with one or two sympathetic key people; then later present it to everyone else as a *fait accompli*.

At the very minimum, the document-writer, like the minute-writer, has immense powers of emphasis and omission.

And the document will seem all the more objective if its author has not declared strong views in advance.

Perhaps because I enjoy writing documents, I'll Write a Document is one of my favourite stratagems.

One of my agency's major clients recently called a large, a depressingly large, meeting to discuss whether or not to press ahead with the launch of a new product on which a lot of development work had been done.

Immediately the pros and antis got stuck into each other, while the don't knows doodled and dreamed.

I wanted the project to proceed. (The agency usually does.) But I held my peace, hoping to be able to swing in heavily in support of the pros as soon as they appeared to be winning.

At no time did they appear to be winning.

After a couple of hours of surge and counter-surge, the antis were beginning to gain ground.

It was now or never.

'Having heard all the arguments aired so clearly,' I unbiasedly interceded, 'perhaps it would be helpful if I wrote a document and maybe came up with a conclusion if there seems to be one.'

The project proceeded.

In addition to document-writing, there are a few other circumstances when it is right and proper to be kindly and charitable and to volunteer for work.

Not many.

But 'I'll do it, then' can occasionally bring satisfaction (and compensation).

There are five known situations when those words can be used sensibly:

* first and foremost, when you know somebody else desperately wants to do it

* when a subordinate is wriggling out of the task, at which point your tone of voice should be sufficiently livid to guarantee that the subordinate immediately wrests the job back from you

* when by enthusiastically offering to take on a tiny task you can escape the much more onerous one you know is going to crop up later

* when you have negligently failed to carry out an important job, or have all too efficiently committed some ghastly gaffe and need to re-establish your credit rating

* when you are certain you won't ever have to do it, either because (a) after the meeting you can delegate it to someone else, or (b) everyone will forget and it will never need to be done.

Meetings being a substitute for work, it is less than logical to allow meetings to cause you lots of extra labours.

'The world is full of willing people,' said American poet Robert Frost, 'a few willing to work, the rest willing to let them.'

The latter being the meeting-goers.

Anyway, with so many meetings to attend, you don't have time for work, do you?

11

It's My Fault It's Your Fault

In its simplest form sometimes called the Pre-emptive Apology, It's My Fault It's Your Fault was first mentioned when we were dealing with the Second Deadly Skill, conciliation.

More complex than most, the complete stratagem is based upon a four-domino psychological sequence: a humble apology stimulates sympathy stimulates guilt stimulates generosity.

That is to say, if my apology can make you feel guilty you will seek subconscious absolution by being nice to me.

(One of the many sound psychological pillars upon which the Catholic confessional has been built.)

Let's take it domino by domino.

I first discovered the power of the Pre-emptive Apology in innocent pre-meeting puberty.

At the age of twelve, cycling jauntily and thoughtlessly on a busy road, I made an unsignalled (and signally unintelligent) U-turn.

A following car thumped my back wheel and I flew gracefully over the handlebars.

When the driver reached me, I, fortunately almost unhurt, apologized profusely for my carefree stupidity – too young to know that the first Rule of the Road (and of the insurance companies) states unequivocally: it's always the other guy's fault.

The driver, who had been fearfully shouting his own defence and accusing me of madness even before he reached me, was struck silent by my naive confession.

Whereupon he began to insist that it was partly his fault for driving too close; that it was partly the sun's fault for having blinded him at that precise moment; that it was partly the road's fault for being too narrow – and, helping me to my feet, gave me £5 to help me mend my bicycle.

A puerile lesson, but never to be forgotten.

Especially not in meetings.

Except that in meetings the aim is to make opponents make the U-turns – from aggression to conciliation.

(Just like the car driver.)

Dale Carnegie once again put the matter cogently:

> 'Say about yourself all the derogatory things you know the person is thinking or wants to say or intends to say – and say them before he has a chance to say them – and you take the wind out of his sails. The chances are a hundred to one that he will then take a generous, forgiving attitude and minimize your mistakes.'

Any fool can try to defend his mistakes – and most fools do – but only the cleverest see the value of the open and undiluted apology.

Having apologized, how do you ensure that your opponent's sympathy is converted into guilt and thence into the milk of human kindness and brotherly love?

To do so, you need to understand guilt's psychological mainsprings.

As we noted (see page 26), Dr Eric Berne describes several marvellous guilt-into-generosity gambits in *Games People Play*; he calls them Pity Me games, and the best are Kick Me, Shlemiel, Wooden Leg, Harried Executive and Lunch Bag (in which the player wins sympathy by taking rough-hewn sandwiches to work every day in a grotty brown paper bag).

However, more recent and more profound work on the subject has been published by B. Latane and J.M. Darley, two of the foremost researchers in the field, and by I. and J. Piliavin and J. Rodin.

Succinctly summarized, their principal relevant findings are:

* individuals are more likely than groups to be helpful and altruistic to those in difficulty

* people are less likely to be helpful if they perceive that somebody more senior, or more capable, is present and should be doing the helping

* people are especially likely to be helpful if they perceive you to be like themselves, i.e. if they can easily identify with your problem

* people are most unlikely to be helpful if you are, in their eyes, a hopeless incompetent and persistently in trouble.

How do these findings apply to meetings?

First, you should aim to arouse guilt in one key target and not aspire to provoke mass self-flagellation.

Second, you should select as your target the person with the greatest authority over the particular problem, who will not necessarily be the most senior person present.

If you select the wrong person, he will shuffle off the problem just as – in psychological projective tests – people fail to go to the rescue of drowning swimmers if they know a life guard is present.

Third, and most important of all, you should consistently associate your target with your own dilemma:

'What would you have done if you'd been me, George?'

'What would you do now if you were me, George?'

(These are among the most powerful and persuasive of all meeting questions, and can be used with great frequency. Note incidentally the precise first-name targeting.)

'I'd greatly appreciate your advice on this, George,'

'You'll know how to solve this mess, I'm sure, George.'

Fourth, you can employ It's My Fault It's Your Fault almost as frequently as you like, but beware of people starting to feel that you're always in hot water.

Unless they are especially saintly – and if they are, what are they doing in meetings? – people get little pleasure from helping fumbling bunglers.

Possibly the greatest all-time player of It's My Fault It's Your Fault was France's late President de Gaulle.

Appearing on national television in his late seventies to explain a presidential blunder, he gazed balefully out at his nation and confessed:

'C'était mon inexpérience.'

After which, he pleaded:

'France, français, aidez-moi.'

– and won another massive majority in the next day's referendum.

12

Ju-jitsu

Like the sport itself, meeting Ju-jitsu comprises a collection of moves and manoeuvres all of which are based upon one tenet: use your opponent's weight and strength to your own advantage.

It is one of the most satisfying stratagems.

Also one of the most difficult.

Passionates and Mums are lousy at Ju-jitsu, Talkies rarely much better; only Seers have the natural instincts necessary.

In meeting Ju-jitsu as in real ju-jitsu (more correctly, of course, called judo) there are many moves, locks and holds.

All demand the same controlled disciplines (analogous to those of the sport):

* never react impetuously to provocation

* spur your opponents into attacking too vociferously, into exaggerating their arguments and pushing them too aggressively

* use the force of your opponents' arguments against them whenever possible.

(Repeating opposing pronouncements word for word when they suit your case is perfect Ju-jitsu.)

Four winning Ju-jitsu moves (which we've given anglicized names stolen from other sports) are Taking the Pitch, Riding the Punch, Skinning the Snake and Sandbagging.

Taking the Pitch comes from baseball (it might be expected to occur in cricket, but doesn't).

The batter decides in advance not to play the next pitch, no matter how tempting.

This seriously unsettles the pitcher.

In meetings, the same effect is achieved by resolving to stay silent and stare quizzically in response to any vituperative attack.

Invariably, the attacker soon starts to belabour you again, with wild punches and disastrous effects to his cause.

A more extreme variety of Taking the Pitch, inapplicable in baseball but perfect for meetings, is to ignore the attack and answer instead an earlier point made by somebody else entirely.

This demands considerable *sang-froid* (not to mention a *soupçon* of *hauteur*).

It can drive a Passionate attacker berserk – part of the art of Ju-jitsu.

Similar to Taking the Pitch, but lacking its premeditation, is Riding the Punch.

Silence, digression and laughter (see Only When They Larf, page 157) are all good punch-riders.

As, in a different way, are the sympathy-winners in It's My Fault It's Your Fault.

(The knack of Riding the Punch is to step backwards, rather than come forward, so that the blow does little harm and the aggressor is unbalanced.)

Skin the Snake is a kids' game in which the players pass through each others' legs and generally get bruised and knocked about in the process.

In meeting Ju-jitsu it is (well, normally) played somewhat differently.

It is more like the negotiating tactic Find a Nit, Pick a Blemish.

First, listen thoughtfully to your antagonist's attack.

(Following Dale Carnegie's saintly and generous advice 'Be a good listener' need not necessarily lead you to respond in ways that are saintly and generous.)

Then dissect his reasoning bit by bit, always starting with the most trivial arguments first, to induce extra rage and rapid exhaustion.

It is equivalent to effecting a painful hold on a finger, ear or toe, as a softening-up prior to a total submission.

To Skin the Snake well, it is often helpful to make notes while your opponent is orating.

This flatters him into feeling that you are taking his arguments seriously, while helping you to keep your cool.

Best of all, it allows you to commence your dissection by claiming, unambiguously, that you have listed several of his points (and it would be best to deal quickly with the least important first).

As in all Ju-jitsu moves, phlegm is essential; the more the others overheat the cooler you must remain.

The fourth Ju-jitsu tactic is Sandbagging.

In poker, the Sandbagger does not bet initially, despite holding strong cards.

Having bluffed weakness, the Sandbagger doubles the stakes once the other players have been suckered into the game.

In meetings, the objects of the tactic are much the same: initially you communicate weakness so that you can thoroughly trounce your antagonists as soon as they come on strong.

(You can now see why it's classified as a Ju-jitsu manoeuvre.)

There are several types of meeting Sandbag.

The 'I'm-totally-undecided-about-that' Sandbag, camouflaging a determined point of view about which you will remain silent until you have the measure of all the opposing arguments.

Then there are the very ordinary negotiating

'I'm-not-at-all-interested-in-buying' and the 'I-just-haven't-enough-money' Sandbags; followed in either case by a swift bid to clinch the deal immediately.

There is the feigned innocent and ignorant 'I-know-nothing-whatsoever-about-this' Sandbag, which tempts opponents to attack loosely and wildly before you deftly send them flying.

There is the bored, doodling 'I'm-not-paying-attention' Sandbag, while you intently await the ideal moment to strike.

Lastly, there is the emotional 'I-don't-care-about-this-issue-at-all' Sandbag, which explodes, apparently inexplicably, into a ferocious rain of blows and karate chops.

No system yet exists for evaluating and honouring skill and success in meeting manipulation.

Nonetheless, if you are sure you have mastered Ju-jitsu, you can modestly award yourself a black belt.

13

Just a Few Charts

Because they are not truly meetings, we shall not be delving deeply into formal lectures and presentations.

In any event, you can find a host of books proffering pontifical words of wisdom on public speaking, academic lecturing and presentation techniques; a few of the best are listed in the bibliography.

However, it is sometimes worthwhile, and exceedingly good fun, to take over a meeting and make a prepared presentation for which nobody but you is prepared.

The stratagem is Just a Few Charts.

Obviously you will need to prepare your visual aids beforehand.

Keep them small – don't let the size of your bag let the cat out.

Keep them few – boil them down to the smallest number possible.

Keep them simple – always essential advice, but especially so when you are aiming to hold the floor without an invitation.

Make sure they will be legible to everyone in the room.

Make sure they look professional but not expensive.

Make sure they're in the right order, and the right way up (remember Kodak's Law, page 17).

Make sure your non-verbal signals are shipshape for the event.

Your voice should be in good, firm, dominant trim; if you've a cold or sore throat, forget it.

You should be dressed your best, so you can confidently take centre stage and be glared at.

At the appropriate moment, tap the table (or catch the chairman's eye), and beg everyone's indulgence 'for just a few moments' as you 'happen to have just a few charts', which you 'hope will put your case clearly'.

Without waiting for a countdown, launch yourself.

From then on, the normal rules of presentation apply.

These ten commandments are based upon W.J. McGuire's important study *The Nature of Attitudes and Attitude Change* (1969):

1. Open by explaining briefly what you are going to say and why.
2. Create the expectation that you are going to solve the audience's problem(s) and/or satisfy the audience's needs.
3. Put the positive case, in terms that are relevant to the audience.

4. Raise and reject the obvious objections.
5. Be continuously responsive to the audience, watch their reactions, e.g. explain points that appear to have been misunderstood.
6. Speak loudly and distinctly, but never sound superior.
7. Control your anxiety, or it will distract your audience and disrupt your message.
8. Accept comments (and even criticisms) seriously and sympathetically, or you will lose the support of even your supporters.
9. Avoid confrontations.
10. At the end, draw the conclusions explicitly, especially conclusions for action.

When you have finished, expect neither applause nor immediate and unanimous agreement.

(You should be so lucky.)

The most common response will be a battle between those you have converted and those you have antagonized.

Try to stay silent and disengage yourself; let your proselytes do the talking.

Only when the issue is nearing its conclusion should you re-enter the fray – (hopefully) for the kill.

Just a Few Charts is another stratagem to use sparingly; if you habitually pull charts out of sacks with the predictability of a conjurer pulling rabbits from his hat, you will rapidly become a meeting leper.

(Which could, as we've mentioned before, be your devious intention.)

If, on the other hand, you spring Just a Few Charts on your colleagues as an occasional special treat, they may well come to welcome it.

Your presentations should be like presents: nice to give, nicer to receive.

14
Let's Vote

Formal votes, in informal get-togethers or even in more formal committees, are nowadays rare. Moreover, they've become strangely distasteful.

People seldom wish to put issues to a vote; you hear chairmen deliberately sidestepping a division, mumbling, 'I'd sooner not take a vote if we can avoid it.'

Perhaps it relates to our democratic and co-operative image of what meetings should be like.

Conventional wisdom postulates that, after a spirited ding-dong debate, everyone should eventually agree about everything, and should depart cheerfully committed to the collective conclusion.

Rather than slouch off feeling fettered and forced to comply with dubious and daft decisions carried by a (stupid/uninformed/prejudiced/childish) majority.

All of which provides a strategic opportunity for meetings manipulators.

The incisive threat of a poll is often sufficient to force weaker, easily embarrassed brethren to accept a course of action they might have preferred to reject.

Clearly this stratagem, Let's Vote, can only be employed
when the outcome of a division is uncertain.

Meetings full of Mums are the perfect stamping ground
for Let's Vote, as nobody can be certain how their favours
will fall.

Likewise, meetings where Passionates are vigorously
slugging each other can often be exploited by deft Let's
Voters.

In an important board meeting, my ex-partner Bill
Shelton, now Minister for Education but then chairman of
our joint company, nimbly outmanoeuvred me by
threatening to call a vote on an issue about which, as he
well knew, tempers were running high.

For my part, as managing director, I was anxious to avoid
a polarization of the board.

I thought the issue serious but not crucial; at the time,
there was a good deal of ill-feeling among the company's
directors which a vote would have further aggravated.

During the discussion, Bill several times threatened a
division; each time, I prevaricated; finally, I backed
down.

As always with threats and bluffs, you must be prepared
for them to be called.

If you keep calling for a vote, your request may eventually
be granted.

In which case, you should know that recent researches on
persuasion and voting behaviour in small groups have
shown that:

* the person who speaks last (i.e., most closely to the vote) has the best chance of winning...

* ... unless the vote is likely to be delayed by, say, a few days, in which case it is best to speak first

* distracting the voters while they are listening to your opponent may, surprisingly, enhance his chance of winning – particularly if his message is a simple one. (He was probably repeating it ad nauseam anyway)

* if you judge the audience to be naive or ill informed, you should never put both sides of the argument: just hit them with your own

* however, if the audience is sophisticated, or is initially against you, you should always present some part of your opponent's case; fail to do so and the audience will believe either that you don't really understand the issue or that you are trying to hide something.

Don't feel that Let's Vote can be played only in large, structured committees.

You'll need to introduce it gently, with a smile, but it works in any group of five or more.

Finally, remember that Let's Vote need not be played as a bluff at all.

If you are truly confident of having the majority's support, call for a vote whenever you fancy.

Just keep in mind that electorates are treacherously fickle, and many an odds-on favourite has been routed in the polling booths.

15

Only When They Larf

'He made humour a tool of diplomacy. His banter
inspired banter in others and usually led to a more
relaxed atmosphere in the private, formal discussions
or negotiations with world leaders. The humour opened
the door to more frankness and less ritualized
recitations as well. In that regard, Kissinger lightened
the whole heavy international diplomatic scene.'

(R. Valeriani, *Travels with Henry*, 1979)

The disarming power of laughter is infamous.

Many an ardent beau has giggled his reluctant belle into
the bedroom.

Just as every great orator peppers his rhetoric with quips
and mockery, and salesmen laugh winningly at even your
feeblest jokes.

It is hardly surprising then that students of social
behaviour have long hypothesized that humour may
facilitate personal influence (e.g. J.D. Goodchild's *On
being witty*, 1972, and T.R. Kane *et al.*, *Humour as a tool
of social interaction*, 1977).

Researches have also unsurprisingly shown that humour

increases the likeability of a communicator (Goodchilds; C. Gruner, 1976; D.R. Mettee *et al.*, 1971); and persuasion studies have consistently indicated that liked communicators are more influential.

However, largely because of the difficulty of propagating genuine and spontaneous mirth under laboratory conditions, the theories were largely supported by circumstantial evidence until the pioneering work of Karen O'Quin and Joel Aronoff in the USA in 1980 (*Social Psychology Quarterly*, Vol. 44, No. 4, 1981).

O'Quin and Aronoff's marvellous experiment was based upon a price negotiation, but clearly relates to all meeting situations.

In the experiment each of one group of subjects was required to sell a painting to each of another group of respondents.

Each pair in turn bargained over the same painting.

All involved were briefed to achieve the best bargain they could, and were told that they would be evaluated on their success as bargainers.

Now for the giggle.

Half the buyers completed their purchase in the normal way saying, 'Well, my final offer is . . . dollars.'

The other half were instructed to smile and say, 'Well, my final offer is . . . dollars, and I'll throw in my pet frog.'

The sellers who were offered the frog made significantly greater financial concessions than those who were not.

More particularly, statistical analysis showed that sellers who laughed at the frog – and not all did – were especially likely to show compliance and accept a lower price.

The result confirms the wisdom of the ages.

If you are aiming to get your own way, make 'em larf.

To help you a bit, another piece of research (H. Leventhal, 1974) proved that people are more likely to laugh if they are prompted by other laughter, even canned laughter.

(He who laughs last has probably just heard someone else chuckling.)

A truth well known to every hack comedian.

So that a little laughter at your own jokes is by no means ridiculous. However, be warned: if you aren't naturally funny never, repeat never, try to be comical in meetings.

Your jests will be as welcome as dishwatery meeting tea.

They'll fall flat, cause embarrassment, make everyone edgy and provoke precisely the opposite response to that sought.

Jokers who aren't amusing are a far greater bane of meeting life than the more infamous chatterboxes and windbags.

On a different tack, there are also occasions to laugh when nothing in the least bit funny has been said.

We noted earlier that derisory laughter can be used scornfully, to suggest the worthlessness of an object being offered for sale (or the foolishness of a proposition being offered as true).

Additionally, and most humorously of all, laughter can be a wonderful response when you are trapped and stumped for an answer – or when there is no answer.

If you have failed to produce a promised document; if you have bungled some simple arithmetic; if you are asked an embarrassing question: laugh.

If you treat the matter as an uproarious joke, then as often as not your antagonist will fold his tent and pretend he was kidding (though he was not).

Laughter can be a devastating defensive weapon.

Use it often.

No matter how counterfeit it sounds to you, roar hilariously.

I have laughed myself out of more scrapes than I can remember.

It's the jolliest way to escape from a jam ever invented by a meeting man.

16
Red Herrings

Lobbing Red Herrings is probably the oldest and commonest of all meeting stratagems.

At its simplest it makes a diverting solitary meeting game, for amusement only.

You gain nothing except a cheering mental chuckle as everyone competes to pickle your herring quickly, but politely, just in case you are serious and might be offended.

The degree of their tongue-tied embarrassment will be a fair measure of the skill with which you lobbed in the fish.

Red Herrings do, however, have more purposeful uses, the prime three being:

– to delay
– to mislead
– to exhaust.

First, delay, the very *raison d'être* of the Red Herring.

To ensure that the meeting does not have time to reach a late item on the agenda, introduce issues about which you know the Passionates care passionately, provoking them like a picador jabbing a bull.

Better still, inject an argument into the proceedings.

The chairman of an advertising agency I once worked for built his business upon injected arguments.

Knowing that his agency was not awfully good at producing advertisements, before each presentation he always briefed himself thoroughly on the conflicting opinions of the client personnel likely to attend.

As the moment when the new advertisements were to be presented approached, but before it came too perilously close, he would incite the clients to start bickering among themselves:

> 'Jim, I know you think the campaign should be national, but John is convinced it should be local, aren't you, John?'

Sometimes the fuse would fizzle out and would need to be re-lit a few times.

The timing of a Red Herring is often crucial: two thirds of the way through the agenda is usually best.

Too early and it is easy for the lost time to be re-couped; too late and people, aware of the lack of remaining time, may refuse to bite the hook.

My chairman, being a deft hand at the manoeuvre, always timed it precisely.

The clients would argue themselves into frenzied

exhaustion. 'They enjoy that,' he claimed, 'it makes them feel they've worked hard and really care.'

Finally, moments before the meeting was to close, he presented the ads. Nineteen times out of twenty they'd be hurriedly accepted, while the participants were still subconsciously scrapping.

The propensity of powerful people to bog themselves down in trivia is the Red Herring's staunchest ally.

Remember C. Northcote Parkinson's rule:

'The time spent on any item of the agenda will be in inverse proportion to the sum of money involved.'

Business mythology is choc-a-bloc with tales of immense multinational company boards of directors who debated the design of the boardroom china so enthusiastically (and endlessly) that the billion-dollar capital investment project had to be authorized in minutes; political meetings regularly argue so interminably over petty procedural points that no time is left for politics.

All triumphs for the Red Herring lobber.

As well as lobbing Red Herrings yourself, you must learn to sniff out other people's and gut them.

Being a stratagem known to all, Red Herrings raise their fishy heads frequently.

Finally, a sub-class, or offspring as it were, of the Red Herring is the Straw Man: the argument of no substance which you don't care a blunt meeting pencil if you lose.

Straw Men, like Red Herrings, delay, mislead and exhaust; but more importantly provide others with cheap victories.

This cheers them up and makes them sympathetic towards you.

As often as not, having won a Straw Man, your opponents will cheerfully lose a crucial argument, vaguely feeling that a fair parity has been achieved.

Of course, Straw Men must not be too obvious, and you must defend them zealously.

You'll need to bring two of the Seven Deadly Skills – aggression and enthusiasm – into full play.

But masterful Straw Men managers win key point after key point while deliberately and noisily giving away nothing at all.

Enter every meeting with a few Red Herrings and Straw Men up your sleeve and you'll never leave empty-handed.

17

Refer It to a Sub

Experienced meeting-goers don't much prize Refer It to a Sub.

It is the most unadventurous, unimaginative and uninspiring of all meeting stratagems.

It is also exceedingly risky since there can be no guarantee that the sub-committee will come to the correct (your) conclusions.

Nonetheless there is a time and place for every stratagem and Refer It to a Sub has its uses.

It is a fine means of procrastination.

If you are in danger of imminent defeat, the snappy creation of a sub will ensure you live to fight another day.

By influencing its membership, you can prejudice its outcome in your favour.

And the most important person to inveigle onto any sub that is going to deal with matters that matter to you is – you.

(Which consequently means you will have to attend still
more meetings; another excellent reason why experienced
meeting-goers aren't crazily keen on the stratagem.)

If you do need to get yourself onto the sub you must not
be backward about coming forward.

In meetings, as we have noted before, shyness and good
manners are wonderful and admirable and guarantee
defeat.

If nobody nominates you, nominate yourself.

Do it properly: make clear that it will be a dreadful extra
burden, that you cannot possibly afford the time, that
fortunately you have complete faith in all the other
nominees, adding humbly that you nonetheless accept the
responsibility and are flattered to have been asked
(whether or not you have been).

As ever, it is crucial to get both the precise formula of
your words and your tone of voice exactly right.

A meeting of one of the Social Democratic Party's senior
national committees upon which I sit recently formed an
important sub-committee upon which I wished to sit.

I was not, in this instance, a party to the party's decision
to form the sub, nor to the decision to limit its
membership to six.

Five of whom were automatically selected by virtue of
their other roles and responsibilities.

Leaving one place open and, as it happened, two possible
contenders.

My competitor, making a pre-emptive bid, piped up first:

'If Winston *really* wants to be on the sub-committee,' he
rasped, glaring at me, 'then that's OK by me.'

Indubitably, politeness and good behaviour dictated that I
should respond, 'No, it's all right, I'm not that keen,'
allowing him to swoop in and grab the tiny trophy.

Instead, I replied firmly, 'That's extremely kind. Yes, I do
really want to, if you don't object terribly.'

Putting him well, truly and satisfyingly in the mire.

However, the membership of important sub-committees
can sometimes elude even the most experienced of
meeting manipulators.

In which case it is often possible, and wise, to castrate the
sub in advance.

First, by proposing that its recommendation be advisory
rather than binding.

(All those who have not been nominated for the sub will
enthusiastically concur.)

Second, by lengthening, widening or simply confusing its
terms of reference.

(It would, after all, surely be unfair and unreasonable to
limit the sub-committee's vision to too narrow a
perspective, forcing it to concentrate on the trees while
losing sight of the wood?)

Third, by proposing that its membership should be an

even number, giving it a goodly chance of reaching a stalemate.

A sub-branch of sub-committee creation is to call in a consultant.

This refinement is usually effective in producing almost indefinite procrastination, plus an eventual report that can never be implemented.

(Herbert V. Prochnow defined a consultant as:

'A man who knows less about your business than you do and gets more for telling you how to run it than you could possibly make out of it even if you ran it right instead of the way he told you.')

Consultants can be guaranteed to confuse and obfuscate any issue, and their ability to do so is directly proportional to the size of their fee.

The only remaining fact you need remember about the use and abuse of sub-committees, and of consultants, can be stated in a few words:

Both are extensively used, all over the world, by governments.

18

Sumpower

An astonishing number of the decisions taken in meetings are based upon inadequate, or even entirely neglected, arithmetic.

Hence it is well worth devoting yourself to the sums while others natter on.

If you are nimble at mental arithmetic, you are at a great advantage; if you're not, carry a calculator.

We're not talking about complex algebraic equations, differential calculus or convoluted balance sheets.

We're referring to plain old simple, but often lengthy, addition, subtraction, multiplication and division.

A director of one of Britain's biggest banks has built his career on such arithmetic.

He sits in meetings checking the sums.

He almost always discovers a few blunders.

A couple of tiny inaccuracies can of course annihilate an otherwise carefully detailed two-hundred-page proposal that has taken months to prepare.

'Back to the drawing board,' cries the bank director jubilantly, even if only the date on the cover is wrong.

This is the less mischievous meeting variety of Dr Eric Berne's famous Now I've Got You, You S.O.B. – in which the player provokes his opponent into making a mistake so that he can then pounce upon him (see also You Won't Fly to the Moon?, page 179).

In meetings, people make so many bloomers of their own accord it is rarely necessary to foment them with malice aforethought.

Alex Bernstein, chairman of Granada, used to employ a similar stratagem based on the certainty of random error – though in this case architectural rather than arithmetical – when first put in charge of his company's new building programme.

'Why is that wrong?' he would ask, pointing to any spot on the architect's plans that caught his eye.

The architect would then be forced to prove that there was no mistake at that particular point.

'Then why is that wrong?' Alex would ask, pointing to another part of the plan entirely.

He repeated the question about seven times; if this failed to reveal a single fault, he generally concluded that all was well.

However, he almost never reached the seventh question on the first or even second occasion the plans were presented; and whenever a mistake was uncovered it was 'Back to the drawing board – and please don't return until you're absolutely and positively certain you've got everything absolutely and positively right.'

As well as checking the arithmetic (or plans) of others, it is beneficial to do the small, neglected sums which arise as the meeting proceeds yourself.

Pointing out the mathematical consequences – which usually means the financial consequences – of any course of action will, at the very least, impress everyone else and score you meeting points.

Sometimes you may win still greater prizes.

I was once at a directors' meeting of a major retail company when the directors agreed that all staff should in future be allowed six pence per day tea and coffee allowance (to buy their beverages from machines).

The company employs some six thousand people.

Although the matter was none of my business, I pointed out that the apparently paltry cost would amount to some £100,000 per year.

Such was everyone's profound gratitude that I was later able to slip through some contentious and costly advertising proposals without debate.

Virtue, even in meetings, is sometimes rewarded.

19

The Sprint

If Red Herrings is the commonest of all the stratagems, and Refer It to a Sub the most unimaginative, then the Sprint is the riskiest.

Sometimes it is called the Vanishing Trick, sometimes I'm Off.

It is withdrawal without the temper.

On arrival, or at a key point in the proceedings, you blandly announce:

> 'Look, I'm awfully sorry but I'm going to have to leave in three minutes.'

(Or even faster if you really seek a stampede.)

Simplicity itself.

However, like withdrawal, and like issuing ultimatums in negotiations, more than a trifle risky.

When then should you dash a Sprint?

First, to throw the opposing forces into chaos and confusion.

Second, to delay the issue, if you can be absolutely
confident no decision will be taken in your absence.

Third, when the argument has been swinging evenly to
and fro, and by forcing the pace, you have a
better-than-evens chance of snatching a snappy victory.

Fourth, when you can foresee your side losing the
argument and do not wish to be party to the debacle.

(You will then be able to blame your erstwhile comrades
for their inept failure: it would never have happened had
you still been there. Ho-hum.)

NB: Deliberate withdrawal must in this case be made
well before the inevitability of your defeat becomes
apparent: to run away when you are clearly on the run is
appalling cowardice and will be universally despised.

Fifth, when you know that the next item on the agenda
will raise matters which you want to avoid – probably
because you have not yet done the work required.

(In which circumstances, it is far better to attend and
leave early, with a strong excuse, than to cut the meeting
altogether.)

Sixth, when you have put forward several ideas, none of
which has been greeted with uproarious enthusiasm, and
now – having run out of ideas – feel no desire to discuss
other people's footling proposals.

Which leads inexorably to the seventh, least
Machiavellian but far and away most frequent, occasion
for a Sprint: when you are bored to distraction and can
stand it no longer.

Or, as occasionally occurs, when the person sitting next to you has dreadful BO.

Being a notorious meeting Sprinter myself, I regularly rush off for any and all of the above reasons.

Most often, admittedly, for the seventh.

Sometimes I later regret it, when the meeting takes daft decisions which – had I but been present – would never have been taken. (Ho-hum again.)

Finally, as with ultimatums, you should never feel a Sprint to be irrevocable.

When you announce you need to leave in three minutes, nobody really believes you; you can easily stay for thirty.

'This is proving to be so vitally important I feel I must hang on.'

Or you can exit, make a mythical phone call to delay your next meeting, and return.

Or you can even go away entirely, pop down the pub for a quick one, and return twenty-five minutes later.

'I left my other meeting as quickly as I could to get back to this crucial discussion.'

In meetings, flexibility and integrity are inextricably intertwined.

And every successful sprinter knows how to run backwards.

20

Trust Me

You are more likely to bend others to your will if they trust you.

A truism that would hardly be news to mankind's great historic leaders – political, military or religious:

'We walk by faith, not by sight.'

(*Corinthians 5:7*)

Unfortunately, the pathetic fact is that you probably lack Napoleon's or Churchill's or Christ's charisma.

Nonetheless, with a little training, and at a lowlier level, you can sweep meetings along with you if they have faith in your leadership.

Cynics call it the gift of the gab.

Psychologists, you will not by now be surprised to learn, have investigated the phenomenon at length and in depth.

C.I. Hovland and W. Weiss in their classic 1951 study *The influence of source credibility on communication effectiveness* proved that, although people remember the facts from trustworthy and untrustworthy sources equally, they are *twice* as likely to be convinced by trustworthy sources.

How can you convince a meeting, particularly of people unknown to you, of your trustworthiness?

First, researches have shown that your trustworthiness will be greatly enhanced if you argue against your apparent self-interest.

'Apparent' being the key word: if you alone know your argument to be self-damaging – which can easily happen – then patently you will score no points.

Second, your trustworthiness will be greatly enhanced if you do not appear to be trying to be persuasive.

People are most often convinced by an argument when they believe the speaker is not trying to convince them.

In one carefully staged experiment, the subjects were more influenced by things they 'accidentally' overheard in a hallway, prior to the experiment, than by the persuasive rhetoric of the speaker.

(Happily, human cussedness reigns supreme.)

Third, people are more likely to accept your arguments if they believe you to be an expert on the subject – despite the sneering scepticism with which the word 'expert' is nowadays commonly used.

One interpretation of the power of the expert is that listeners are rational folk modestly seeking truth.

A less idealistic interpretation (J.M. Jellison, 1974) is that experts cause people to lose confidence in their own judgements.

Whatever the reason, it is clearly advantageous to establish your expertise at the outset.

If you've a doctorate or a relevant title (financial director or production manager or whatever), make sure everyone knows about it. (Do not, however, invent titles, or somebody will demolish you with a Blusher.)

If, sadly, you lack official recognition of your expertise, you must insinuate it more subtly.

Subtlety is important because fourth, and finally, researches have unequivocally proved that experts who act overconfidently and appear 'cocky' have their views rejected.

(Life is not all bad news.)

By now it will probably be obvious that it is easier to make those who know you less trust you more.

'I don't trust him. We're friends,' as Brecht perceptively pointed out in *Mother Courage*.

Maybe it is simply a symptom of that notorious human ailment diagnosed by doctors as *Grassus greeneris fieldus nextii*; maybe it is inevitable that as people get to know us they discover our failings and feet of clay.

Either way the outcome is the same: you will more often win a meeting's trust if you are a convincing stranger than if familiarity has bred contempt.

A corollary of this is that when you play Trust Me you must hold your cards close to your chest.

The more you say, the more you give away, the more people will find to argue with, the more your image will be dented.

So the perfect play for Trust Me runs: be a quietly confident expert, arguing against yourself to a group which hardly knows you.

Not always easy, admittedly.

(But then you can hardly hope to be a great charismatic leader without putting in a little effort.)

21

You Won't Fly to the Moon?

Not all human beings are boasters, but the multitudes who are adore meetings passionately.

Doubtless they find such delectable opportunities to display their infinite wit and wisdom too irresistible to resist.

Doubtless you've noticed.

Psychologists describe these less-than-modest folk as having a high nAch – nAch being their need for achievement as measured by the TAT (Thematic Apperception Test), devised in the late 1930s by Henry Murray at Harvard.

High nAch people avoid tasks which are too simple and which therefore provide little challenge; likewise, they avoid tasks which are too difficult, as they have an innate fear of failure.

(Recognize any high nAchers among your regular meeting-going gang?)

Even without getting everyone to take a TAT on arrival, which may not always be convenient, you can quite easily differentiate high nAchers from low nAchers.

The high nAchers brag more. (Nachurally.)

Happily, this means that manipulating them is as easy as twisting paperclips.

They can always be coaxed into putting their case too strongly and committing themselves to too much.

First you draw them into a commitment with the kind of classic cue no high nAcher can ignore:

> 'You'll never do that in the time, Harold.'

> 'Do you really have the experience to tackle anything so complicated, Vera?'

> 'I just don't believe your little company has the skill or resources to cope with the order, Mr Fanshawe-Smythe.'

Having set the bait, there are several ways to snap the trap.

At the minimum you simply let them pick up the challenge and press on, since you are already in a win-win situation.

If they succeed, you congratulate them warmly saying, 'I bet you're grateful I goaded you into pushing yourself that bit further.'

If they fail, it's I-told-you-so time again.

However, it is more fun, and you strengthen your win-win position, if you can sucker them into small but onerous additional commitments.

The straws must be loaded onto the camel's back
patiently, one by one; remember that, if you try to toss
impossibly high bales onto high nAchers, they shake
themselves free of the entire load.

The stratagem must – to take another analogy – be played
like a strong poker hand: you can keep pushing the other
players to put pennies into the pot, but if you call a
colossal raise there is a fair chance they'll fold.

(Especially if they are high nAchers.)

Thus the follow-ups go something like:

> 'That's wonderful, Harold, but looking at the detail I
> now see it'll be needed twenty-four hours earlier. Are
> you still sure ... ?'

> 'Tremendous, Vera, you realize of course we won't be
> able to provide any computer time back-up, so are you
> certain you'll be able to cope ... ?'

> 'Impressive indeed, Mr Fanshawe-Smythe; by the way,
> had you noticed that the order is even bigger than it
> seems, when you add it all up ... ?'

By now Harold, Vera and Mr Fanshawe-Smythe are in for
a penny, in front of (as they think, being high nAchers) an
awestruck, admiring audience – so they might as well be
in for another penny.

And another: you might perhaps lob time constraints at
Vera and Mr Fanshawe-Smythe, and throw a nice
production pickle into Harold's little lot.

If you have played the stratagem well, then Harold, Vera
and Mr Fanshawe-Smythe should leave the proceedings
as pleased with themselves as can be.

Only in the middle of the cold night should they wake in a shivering sweat, realizing the magnitude of the task they have undertaken.

(Though many boasters are impervious to worry and will snore confidently the whole night through.)

I once witnessed the stratagem played delightfully at a large meeting in a small computer company.

The sales director was a high nAching bullshitter of the finest quality.

He committed himself to breaking into any and every new market mentioned.

Finally, one of his colleagues asked earnestly whether it might not be a good idea to contact NASA, in order to secure the first available lunar hardware contract.

The sales director, by now flying on automatic pilot, responded enthusiastically: 'Worth a try, never say die.'

'Well, you'd better make damn sure you've booked on the first spaceship that goes,' the managing director joined in, 'I don't damn well want to hear IBM have beaten us to it again.'

The sales director grinned cheerfully if inanely but at last said nothing.

'You mean you're going to let us down on this one?' the managing director grunted, 'you mean, You Won't Fly to the Moon?'

Any Other Business

Why is mankind so addicted to meetings?

Why is the world so full of meetingolics?

(Meetingolics are otherwise normal people who have
become meeting-dependent and suffer withdrawal
symptoms – lassitude, irritability, anxiety, indecision and
even morose depression – when starved of their daily fix
of fixtures.)

The questions have baffled philosophers since the dawn of
time, and psychologists since psychology was invented.

Man is a social animal, claimed Aristotle.

Only by coming together in groups can humanity avoid
mutual self-destruction, claimed Hobbes.

('Jaw, jaw is better than war, war.')

Group formation is just an instinct surviving from the
primal hordes of primitive man, claimed Sigmund Freud.

Meetings are just a way of avoiding work, claims my
brother Martin.

Humans who are totally isolated grow into freaks; and hermits are generally believed to be batty.

Yet none of this quite explains why the world's population deems it necessary to get together in 50 million little gatherings each and every day.

It's a riddle wrapped in a mystery inside an enigma.

It's an appalling waste of one of humanity's scarcest resources: time.

To solve the problem, I believe the world should set up an investigative committee.

(Of dedicated committee-goers, naturally.)

I would like to be one of its members myself, but unfortunately can't spare a moment.

I'm disgracefully late for my next meeting already.

BIBLIOGRAPHY

The many research studies and reports referred to in the text are to be found, in greater detail, in the books below – particularly in those of Professor Michael Argyle, and in the textbooks and collections of readings by Robert C. Beck, Paul V. Crosbie, and Harold Koontz, Cyril O'Donnell and Heinz Weinrich.

ARGYLE, MICHAEL, *Social Interaction*, Tavistock, London (1969).

ARGYLE, MICHAEL, *The Psychology of Interpersonal Behaviour*, Pelican, London (1978).

ARGYLE, MICHAEL, *The Social Psychology of Work*, Pelican, London (1972).

ARGYLE, MICHAEL, and THROWER, PETER, *Person to Person*, Harper & Row, London (1980).

BACK, KEN and KATE, *Assertiveness at Work*, McGraw-Hill, Maidenhead, Berkshire (1982).

BECK, ROBERT C., *Applying Psychology, Understanding People*, Prentice-Hall, New Jersey (1982).

BERNE, ERIC, *Games People Play*, Ballantine, New York (1964).

BRADBURY, MALCOLM, *The History Man*, Arrow, London (1975).

BRADFORD, LELAND P., *Making Meetings Work*, University Associates, California (1976).

BUSKIRK, RICHARD, *Handbook of Management Tactics*, Hawthorn, New York (1976).

CARNEGIE, DALE, *How to Win Friends and Influence People*, Cedar, Tadworth, Surrey (1938).

COHEN, HERB, *You Can Negotiate Anything*, Bantam, New York (1980).

CROSBIE, PAUL V., *Interaction in Small Groups*, Macmillan, New York (1975).

DOUGLAS, MARY, *Witchcraft Confessions and Accusations*, Tavistock, London (1970).

DOYLE, MICHAEL, and STRAUS, DAVID, *How To Make Meetings Work*, Playboy Press, Chicago (1976).

DRUCKER, PETER F., *The Effective Executive*, Pan Piper, London (1966).

DRUCKER, PETER F., *The Practice of Management*, Pan Piper, London (1955).

FABER, HAROLD, *The Book of Laws*, Sphere, London (1980).

FAST, JULIUS, *Body Language*, Pan, London (1978).

FARNSWORTH, TERRY, *On The Way Up*, McGraw-Hill, Maidenhead, Berkshire (1976).

FISHER, ROGER, and URY, WILLIAM, *Getting To Yes*, Hutchinson, London (1981).

FLETCHER, WINSTON, *The Admakers*, Michael Joseph, London (1973).

GOFFMAN, ERVING, *Interaction Ritual*, Allen Lane The Penguin Press, London (1967).

GOODWORTH, CLIVE, *Effective Speaking and Presentation*, Wyvern Business Library, Ely, Cambridgeshire (1980).

HALL, L., *Meetings*, M&E Handbooks, Plymouth, Devon (1977).

HELLER, ROBERT, *The Business of Winning*, Sidgwick & Jackson, London (1980).

HON, DAVID, *Meetings That Matter*, Wiley, New York (1980).

INSTITUTE OF DIRECTORS, *Standard Boardroom Practice*, Institute of Directors, London (1968).

JAY, ANTONY, *Management and Machiavelli*, Hodder & Stoughton, London (1967).

JENNINGS, EUGENE EMERSON, *The Executive*, Harper & Row, New York (1962).

JONGEWARD, DOROTHY, *Everybody Wins*, Addison Wesley, California (1976).

KOONTZ, HAROLD, O'DONNELL, CYRIL, and WEINRICH, HEINZ, *Management*, McGraw-Hill, New York (1980).

LOCKE, MICHAEL, *How To Run Committees and Meetings*, Macmillan, London (1980).

MACKAY, COLIN NEIL, *Speak For Yourself*, Directors Bookshelf, London (1971).

MARTIN, THOMAS L., *Malice in Blunderland*, McGraw-Hill, New York (1973).

MAUDE, BARRY, *Managing Meetings*, Business Books, London (1975).

PAGE, MARTIN, *The Company Savage*, Coronet, London (1972).

PARKINSON, C. NORTHCOTE, and ROWE, NIGEL, *Communicate*, Pan, London (1977).

POTTER, STEPHEN, *Gamesmanship*, Hart-Davis, London (1947).

POTTER, STEPHEN, *Lifemanship*, Hart-Davis, London (1950).

POTTER, STEPHEN, *One-Upmanship*, Hart-Davis, London (1952).

PRINCE, GEORGE M., *The Practice of Creativity*, Collier, New York (1970).

RAWLINSON, J. GEOFFREY, *Creative Thinking and Brainstorming*, Halsted Press, New York (1981).

REEVES, ELTON T., *The Dynamics of Group Behavior*, American Management Association, New York (1970).

SCHEFLEN, ALBERT E., *Body Language and Social Order*, Spectrum, New Jersey (1972).

SCOTT, BILL, *The Skills of Negotiating*, Gower Press, Aldershot, Surrey (1981).

SINGER, ERIC, *A Manual of Graphology*, Duckworth, London (1974).

SINGER, ERIC, *Personality In Handwriting*, Duckworth, London (1974).

SWOPE, GEORGE S., *Interpreting Executive Behavior*, American Management Association, New York (1970).

TAYLOR, HENRY, *The Statesman*, Mentor, New York (1936).

TOWNSEND, ROBERT, *Up The Organization*, Michael Joseph, London (1970).

WEBSTER, ERIC, *How To Win The Business Battle*, John Murray, London (1964).

WINKWORTH, STEPHEN, *Great Commercial Disasters*, Macmillan, London (1980).

Plus original research reports and studies from academic journals detailed in the text.